I DID THIS FOR YOU

One Woman's Journey to Become
A Voice for the Voiceless in the
Northern Ireland Residential Care System

Margaret Mary McGuckin

Printed in Ireland.

Book edited by Susan McKenna (www.bookhubpublishing.com)
Reviewers: Susan McKenna/Karen Gallen
Cover design by Dorothy Dreyer

ISBN – Paperback : 978-1-7392899-5-9

First Edition : 2023

'Nobody's Child' Songwriters: Cy Coben / Mel Foree
Nobody's Child lyrics © Sony/ATV Music Publishing LLC, Warner
Chappell Music, Inc

Photo of Margaret McGuckin on title page from Margaret's personal family collection
taken at the Aisling Awards Ceremony where she was chosen from all entries as final
'Person of the Year' for her many years as a Social Activist campaign lobbying for Justice for
Survivors and victims of Institutional Abuse.

Dedication

This book is dedicated to the thousands of children across the globe who, coming through the care system; - whether that be of being resident in care settings of orphanages, care homes, training schools or in any Institutionalised facility run by the churches, the religious orders or the state – have suffered horrendously. Particularly for those who after suffering from the severe traumatic after-effects of Institutional abuse and neglect, went on to live a life filled with yet more darkness and despair. I understand and know first-hand, that many were forced to live in society with an abject fear and mistrust of those around them, being wrongly deprived of the natural human right to flourish with expectations and hope for a brighter future. This is also in memory of those who have passed on without receiving any form of justice or restitution, in that what they may have suffered is now out in the public domain, through the words of fellow ex-residents. And for those who can now believe that they, too, have a voice and can be heard, just be persistent and relentless, refuse to back down, refuse to keep quiet or to go away, continue to speak out for the most vulnerable until listened to. I also dedicate this book to those who cannot or are unable to speak up for themselves - just like Kevin, my dear long-suffering brother, who after being led like a lamb to the slaughter was taken advantage of, as a very young child behind the walls of a supposedly safe place. Kevin was used and abused in the vilest manner, into his teenage years by some of those who were supposed to be his carers and friends, in many care institutions. No longer a part of mainstream society, he has spent a lifetime in the' care system'. Authority figures have been so wrong in making decisions on his behalf. Kevin is now past middle age and finally in a much safer place; a nursing home, with more loving care and attention to his needs. I thank the nursing staff also. I dedicate this book to you, Kevin.

Acknowledgements

I would like to sincerely thank those who encouraged me over the many years to write this book, those who believed in me and supported me throughout my writing as I began to finally do so. My three sons, Steven, James and John, my family that I can now truly call my own. To Peter my brother and for my sister Bernie, Onwards and upwards.

My grandson Steven and granddaughter Cara-Margaret, I love you all. I feel much freer now having released this lifelong burden. Thank you, my boys, for your support and belief in my writing even though you didn't and don't know, the true reality of what I was going to uncover. So much so, I haven't revealed it all as I don't want you boys to ever feel any hurt the way I did. I'm ok now, ok. I'm so proud of you all, still like my young children to me, just as I feel I am myself, a child who hasn't really had a chance to grow up into maturity, or to live life as it should be...one day perhaps, one day!

The HIA victims and survivor's services (VSS) Nicola Nugent specifically, who listened and genuinely wanted to hear me. She reassured me that what I was coming through was indeed trauma, a result of holding all my pain inwardly and not releasing it. Nicola got to know me better than I knew myself. She professionally understood my moods and when I was low or hysterical assured me that I wasn't going mad or psychotic; it was a diagnosis of PTSD. Because of her, I began to open up more freely and to put it down of paper. Thank you, dearest Nicola.

Also, many thanks to my new friend, Lucinda Dougan who is always a friendly face and a breath of fresh air to have around. Lucinda of Advice NI working with VSS and SAVIA helped in so many ways. She took time out of her normal job setting to visit me whilst I was going through the process of writing. Thank you, Lucinda.

Thanks to Rosie of V&S also. It took a while for us to get to know one another, but now I feel we have done just that, and I am grateful for your kindness and understanding of my ways and situations.

Thanks too to the Wave Trauma Centre; Sandra Peake and Alan McBride, who have been friends of mine in support of our SAVIA campaign and their own Victims of the NI Troubles campaign, whom I've always supported throughout many long years.

I'm eternally grateful for having my faith in later life; my personal non-denominational relationship in Him. Without having my faith I wouldn't be where I am today. I certainly wouldn't have been able to have had the energy and unlimited motivation to have campaigned for fifteen years, without Him by my side. Thank you, Jesus, for your encouragement to me daily and forever - just to be strong and courageous!

For my mentors and those who prayed for me whilst campaigning, Brendan and Angela McCauley and family, John and Trish Edwards, John and Elaine Duffy, Terry and his dearly beloved late wife Gerri Hogg. Johann and Andrea Vizagie, Owen and Anne Crane, Ros and Steve Critchlow.

To Susan McKenna, Director and Commissioning Editor at Book Hub Publishing and to her Team for their editing suggestions and work with me over the past year on my book.

Thank you all. Margaret

Endorsements

"Margaret McGuckin is the embodiment of speaking truth to power. Her bravery and commitment to keep going despite the obstacles put in her way – of which there were many – is incredible. In a campaign that lasted over fifteen years, and with a lifetime of carrying around the terrible abuse she suffered as a child, Margaret never took no for an answer, and constantly put the needs of others ahead of her own. An incredible woman with an incredible story."

—Anna Mercer, Deputy Director, Stratagem; political advisor to
SAVIA

"I am privileged to have met many remarkable people. Margaret is among the Premier League of individuals whom I admire for their courage, determination and refusal to bow down to authority. What is all the more remarkable is that she does it for others, not herself. She is a relentless and selfless leader for those who suffered the double indignity of being abused and then ignored. It is both an honour and an education to know and support her."

—Mike Nesbitt, MLA for Strangford

"Margaret McGuckin's book tells the powerful account of a child who grew up stigmatised in a children's home who became the woman who took on the Government and won. Without her, the abuse neglect of a generation of children locked up in church and state institutions would never have been known. In her relentless campaign she truly found her calling. She is an inspiration to rights activists who speak for the underdog. Her honest no-nonsense approach had the most esteemed and experienced of officials shivering in their shoes. In the 15 year fight for Redress for Survivors of child abuse, I was fortunate to find in this remarkable woman a mentor and friend who has done an unprecedented service for survivors and victims throughout this country."

—Claire McKeegan Solicitor

"Into the bleak bureaucracy of a stalled Stormont marched the inimitable Mags, a one-woman Belisha Beacon lighting up the dark corners of Ireland's awful past. Her redemptive story, told, amazingly, without rancour, gives a voice to the many children thrown to those clerical wolves in sheep's clothing who turned sanctuaries into slaughterhouses. Her words deserve not just to be read but to be appended to every church missalette and nailed to the door of every government ministry charged with the care of our vulnerable children. Preach it, Mags."

—Máirtín Ó Muilleoir,
MD Belfast Media Group & Irish Echo

"Margaret took on the establishment and won, she refused to believe any door was closed to her and the victims whose cases she championed. Her personal story is a harrowing one, but her past has not defined her future. A powerhouse of a woman she has carried out her campaign work at all times with dignity and poise. To steal a quote from Shakespeare "Though she be but little she is fierce.""

—Allison Morris, Journalist Belfast Telegraph
and formally with the Irish News.

"This book exposes the sheer hypocrisy of invoking divine and state authority to subject vulnerable children, sisters and brothers, to institutional regimes of deprivation, isolation and punishment. As a child Margaret McGuckin endured profound personal suffering of what amounted to incarceration. As an adult she has dedicated her life to exposing decades of immunity exploited by those responsible. Her resilience, courage and determination to reveal the truth and secure justice for thousands of survivors has never wavered."

—Professor Phil Scraton, School of Law, Queen's University Belfast,
co-author of Truth, Acknowledgement and Accountability:
Mother and Baby Institutions, Magdalene Laundries
and Workhouses in Northern Ireland.

Contents

FOREWORD

Margaret McGuckin is a force of nature. Her campaign along with other victims' groups, to get justice for victims of institutional child abuse in Northern Ireland lasted decades and faced endless delays and hurdles along the way. When I first met Margaret and the other victims' groups, I was appalled at how their childhood trauma had been reignited time and time again by those in power who had in their gift the ability not to erase their experiences but to acknowledge them and compensate them and above all publicly confirm to victims that nothing in their abuse was their fault. I was determined to do everything I could to bring things to a head. Margaret was such a key part of delivering justice and payments to victims.

Margaret's book exposes in stark terms the true horror of what happened in Children's homes throughout Northern Ireland. Childhood innocence ripped apart by those religious and charitable groups trusted to care for them in loco parentis. Even when the apologies to victims came in 2022, they were often muted and muffled by the weight of legal checks that they had gone through. Margaret and the thousands of other victims of institutional child abuse were let down terribly by many people, people trusted and respected in their public lives.

This book is a stark reminder of the nightmare of what occurred and how every case of child abuse wreaks havoc for a lifetime. It also exposes the importance of why listening to victims and acting to help and support them is a duty on all of us who have been fortunate to have had a childhood of innocence and not abuse.

MARGARET MCGUCKIN

For Margaret, writing these experiences in her memoir has not been easy, but she has triumphed to document them for the record, just as she has triumphed in overcoming obstacles to shine a light from darkness to truth.

—Rt Hon Julian Smith CBE, former Secretary of State for Northern Ireland

WHY THIS BOOK?

'I Did It For You' details my poignant memoir that seeks to shed light on the emotional and psychological ramifications of growing up amidst the trauma and profound challenges of St. Nazareth's Institution and the enduring impact it has had on my life and the lives of so many others. My hope is that through genuinely heartfelt prose, I have faithfully remembered events and characters and chronicled my journey from a young child to now, navigating along the way, the very complex labyrinth of residential child care as it once was in Northern Ireland.

This book is an exploration of the emotional turmoil, resilience, and eventual healing that comes from living with the aftermath of this early childhood trauma. It provides a deeply personal account of my experiences, while also offering a broader understanding of the systemic issues prevalent within the residential care system so that others may come to know some of what we experienced as children and teens in care. And, there were many of us.

I write about our loss of innocence, the longing for stability and familial connection, and the indomitable spirit that allows human beings to survive such adversity. The book also explores the lasting impact of childhood trauma, including the challenges faced, throughout our lives in developing trusting relationships, managing emotions, and finding a sense of belonging inside and outside the walls of such horrid, harsh and unforgiving institutions.

Ultimately, my memoir highlights the crucial importance of advocacy and reform within the residential child care system and the roles politicians and those in power must continue to take in assisting and driving this process. It encourages everyone to take time to reflect on the importance of providing safe and nurturing environments for children, promoting awareness and understanding.

Finally, it takes to task those in authority who were entrusted with our care. Those who failed so miserably. Again and again and again.

CHAPTER ONE

I find myself standing yet again, staring out my windows, watching life go by something I often tend to do. This addictive trait has occurred habitually since my 'release' from Nazareth House Institution in Northern Ireland, a facility run by Religious Orders. I'm now in my early sixties, with my children all grown up and flown the nest. Why am I constantly doing this? What am I looking out for? What, or who, am I hoping to see? Am I expecting someone to come knocking and, once again, take me away from this house, like every house I've ever been in? Is this why I keep moving house every few years, never allowing myself to settle down? Always on the run, thinking in my childlike mind that no one will ever find me if I just keep moving around?

It's time to completely unload this heavy burden within me. I've carried this for so long; it has become much too painful and soul-destroying to take it any further.

I now feel like a pressure cooker about to explode, with the lid about to lift off with an undercurrent akin to an explosive eruption. I cannot allow the lid to close or cover up ever again. I now need to release what I've stored up inside the deep caverns of my being, and pray in doing so, that it will help me to believe I am no longer a prisoner of the past and to finally reassure me...that I am indeed free!

Four walls without a visible escape route drag me back in time, drawing me into an instant panic of distress, anxiety, and fear! Freedom? I desire and need to be free from within this confinement, from any barriers that seemingly hold me in.

Even though the walls surrounding me are barriers in my mind, they are walls of fear-filled memories of so long ago. Walls that locked me in and from which I couldn't escape. They only remind me of the walls that attempted to hide away a multitude of sins, wrongdoing, and horrendous abuses of all descriptions, including, physical, emotional, spiritual abuse and neglect. How can I ever be free from these crippling fears; tormented by these unwanted memories in the night? These dreams of ungodly creatures dressed in dark, black hooded-like robes that seemingly follow me. Visions of these almost spectre-like figures scuttling by, their hauntingly echoing footsteps sending soundings out, likened to an early warning system of doom, letting us know they are on the way back! Their uniformed statuette figures seem to float and hover aimlessly in the eerie cold dark corridors, heads bent with arms folded around the fronts of their long black frocks. Menacing, repetitive swishing noises, echo in the distance as the long black garments sweep along the hallways, all held together by thick leather belts that are overlong, dropping down to one side.

We had become accustomed to and very familiar with this belt, having been beaten with it so often. Heavy black and orange rusty-coloured keys often attached to this belt, which, on occasion, served as a weapon depending on what came to their hands quickest. Noticeable are their white-knuckled hands, those usually hidden away under the black pouch like a covering apron that sits over their frocks. Hands and fingers clasped tightly together, with their most sacred rosary beads intertwined around each finger and thumb.

Every morning, evening, and night they religiously pray their repetitive monologues of the rosary. Over and over, the same prayers are said as their fingers move from one bead to another, again and again, hoping that as they get to the end of this process, God will be pleased with them. Sadly, they believe that if they pray faster and longer and hold the beads tighter, they imagine they are connecting with God! Meaningless!

And to think how they awoke us, children, very early in the morning, forcing us to get down on bended knees to pray or repeat repetitive man-made words that meant nothing to us. This same ceremony was enacted again at night, prayer before eating, sleeping, and immediately after awakening. So-called prayers only terrified us and left us in fear of this strange and angry God that they supposedly adored and worshipped yet gave us nightmares. So strange and eerie.

This real-life spectacle often occurred throughout the days and evenings as we children watched, constantly peeping around corridor walls, knowing when they were coming out of the chapel built within the walls of the Convent. Then, after their time praying on their knees to God, whom they told us was very angry and who made us feel hated, we were told that sinners and us children would burn in Hell because 'we were the mortal-sin carrying children, of sinful mothers.' This name-calling wasn't accurate, even if we had parents who had only fallen on hard times. The nuns held their anger in having to spend their precious prayer time attempting to look after us 'waifs and strays.' So hard to be rid of these images. No escape from them.

Suddenly, a burst of bright, late autumn hazy sunshine dazzles me, bringing me back into the present, warming and comforting, reassuring me, letting me know that all is well and that I'm still free. Looking outwards from my living room window, I'm drawn to my colourful plants and am immediately brought back to my earliest memories of happier family times in childhood. I see the contents of my little garden, still blooming, beautiful, and bright, just like way back then. A long, long time ago. These are fond and happy reminders of many years ago that spring up. Happy memories which bring a smile to my face and a warm glow to my heart. A feeling of comfort, security and happiness. A time back then, when I once belonged to and lived in a caring family home filled with laughter, warmly wrapped in a cosy, secure feeling of being loved and of belonging.

I'm watching the early evening sun still shining down from above, pouring out its heat upon some of the remaining flowers that weakly but determinedly stand tall. Pretty faces and petals are almost hidden as my little flowers peep out from behind larger overbearing darker evergreens. A range of flowers still insistent in keeping their heads held high, looking up to the sun, breathing in its last warm rays of late sunshine.

In doing so, they hang on to life, doggedly refusing to lay down and die, knowing if they, at least, get through this latest cold spell, they will yet again arise, survive and become stronger than ever before. Miracles will still take place even though the flowers may die off and drop down into the soil and disappear. This metamorphosis, likening to the sowing and reaping of seeds buried underneath in darkness, though after going through this process of stillness and seemingly death, they will spring up with a regenerative growth once again. They will live to fight through many more uncertain seasons ahead.

The much stronger evergreens that were once miniature pine and fir trees now grow gracefully, proudly and confidently upright with a knowing that each one will remain standing singly and together in their fight to exist. Nature gives all a built-in instinct to survive the storms and chaos of life. No matter what one comes through, if one is able to stand tall, stay strong and fight for survival, then one will most certainly live!

I'm watching closely now, as my most vulnerable flowers and shrubs continue to attempt to blossom in their deepest desire to survive, throughout this latest struggle and the changing over of seasons. This, even though they know their time is almost up, knowing in a short while so many around them also, will be no more. The fierce onslaught of a harsh and life-taking winter takes a stranglehold on the weakest and most frail.

These musings reflect the context of the lives of many survivors and victims of institutional abuse in my experience. Year in and out, some live, but sadly so many just haven't the strength to continue, to hang on; they give up, having nothing nor no one to support them, to encourage them, or to look up to. The cruel and savage attacks and abusive behaviour they went through, years of severe assaults upon them in the darkness, already damaged their mentality and means to carry on. It all took its toll on them; they were unable to survive or live life outside of institutional walls, to go through perhaps yet more of the coldness and harshness of the unknown or whatever lay ahead. This is because they believed what they were told when in care, that they were 'no good', they were 'unwanted rejects', and so they gave in to what was spoken over them, almost daily or weekly, the belief grew in that they, we, could never survive and that one's life was, indeed, meaningless.

A dark depression overtakes many of us, tempting us and drawing us to give up and die. With no desire within us to rise up and fight for our lives, many have preferred to go into their shells of protection, to be no more, rather than risk yet more of the beatings and humiliation in this world, a world without love and protection. Thinking that to do so, will take the pain and memories away, believing that by giving up the fight they not feel the pain of rejection any longer.

Involuntary, happier early childhood memories spring up of flowers mixed with the sweet aroma of a wallflower, night-scented stock, sweet pea, and honeysuckle, my instantly visualising the homegrown vegetables, carrots, onions, potatoes and rhubarb that my father and mother had planted and grown in the back and side garden of our former family home.

A rickety garden shed which stood by the wall packed with a watering can, tools, spades, and rakes, leaning against each other whilst spanners, hammers, and tools of all kinds, are stacked high up on shelves, this provided a perfect hideaway for small children to play in mischievously, once father's eyes were not on them. A place of exploration for us wee ones to be, now able to walk alone within the boundaries of the parental home. A new world of discovery and of finding treasures never having noticed or known of them ever before in our infancy.

Our family home was surrounded by green fields and steep banks that led down to a large black pipe or tunnel built into either side of the riverbanks, which stretched over the running river below. A river, fast flowing at times, with little rocks that my father and older siblings used as stepping-stones to hesitantly lead us hand by hand across from one side to the other. My father always carried me as I was the youngest, the baby of our family of four; two boys and two girls. I recall feeling so special at those moments. I felt protected and loved. My sister once mentioned to me that I had been spoiled and bought some beautiful outfits like my berry red fur coat with attached mittens, bonnet and accessories to match. Something that she remembered so well in later life, jokingly reminding me that I was a spoilt brat. This exciting, adventurous way of travel, cutting through fields and overgrown marshes, was a shortcut to the local shops and, in particular, the local home bakery that sold freshly baked buns, soda farls and soft potato bread.

The cul-de-sac where we lived in our corner three-bedroomed house angled onto two bungalows, which lay above a steep grassy embankment leading to the picturesque river below.

I recall being outside on the square watching my brothers and sister play and carrying my favourite pet, my kitten, in my arms, protecting it from a barking dog, not knowing why this dog should come after the kitten or me. I ran with the kitten and shooed the dog away, never letting go of this defenceless creature. I kept it safe from the growling dog, which bared its teeth at us both, although the snarling dog did manage to eventually bite me and made the fingers of my left-hand bleed. But my kitten was safe; I wasn't ever going to allow a bullying dog to attack a vulnerable little animal, never mind myself being mauled. I started facing up to my adversaries at a very young age, it seemed. I didn't know then what lay ahead for me – standing up for people and also protecting animals. I was in training mode at that very early stage of my life in preparation for the years to come as a grown adult. I just wasn't aware of it at the time. A child, barely old enough to comprehend in any shape or form the ways of the world and its structures, a world in which I very soon would have to step into and begin the struggle to survive against all the odds stacked against me.

When I was three and a half years old, my mother left the family home, and my father was raising me, my sister and two brothers, alone. My father was a working man, either a lorry driver or a bus driver, parking his lorry outside our home in the parking bay. He continued to work as it was the only way he could afford to feed and clothe his young family and pay off a mortgage and various bills. As dad worked and our eldest sister and brother looked after us wee ones, I'm sure the neighbours noticed the disappearance of our mother and that we were alone.

I'm not sure how the schooling situation went for my elder siblings. They had formerly been going to a primary school in the Drumbo area, though now, because our mother left, the authorities had been informed by someone. This most likely, I believe, was the reason that the State of Northern Ireland Welfare Department and the Catholic Church intervened and decided to remove myself and my siblings from my father and our once-happy family home and place us into the 'care' of the Sisters of Nazareth.

This was the worst decision ever that could have been made on our behalf. The decision of these lawmakers, government, and church religious leaders destroyed our family and our relationship as brothers and sisters forever! We lost each other in the process. We had all been separated immediately as we were driven to the Institutions by those who promised my father that they would look after us and could do a better job of this than our dad. How wrong they were. We were now deprived of our father already having been deprived of our mother, but now we were losing each other as brothers and sisters! Our whole family, once complete, had now been pulled apart, literally!

I vaguely remember my father getting us ready to leave the family home. We were all put into our downstairs bathroom, our elder sister assisting with our final bath before getting us dressed. We all were seated down to eat our dinner, laid out on our little square wooden fold-up table, covered in brightly coloured small smartie-like circular shapes, a table that dad had made himself. We always played 'guess what colour' games, as we placed our little fingertips upon the dots, as we guessed which colour was beneath. Fond memories.

Alas, unknown to us, this would be our last mealtime together in our happy family home surroundings. On leaving our home, our front door closed tightly behind us; little did we know we would never return to live permanently under my dad's roof.

Suddenly we were in a gloomy arch-shaped alcove, standing at a weather-beaten brown door. We had arrived at the infamous Nazareth House Convent run by the Religious Orders. This large Institution on the outskirts of Belfast housed elderly people, young toddlers, and older children up to the

11

age of fifteen who had been placed into their care. All were situated in separate wings of the home. An old, corded bell was built into a small hatch within the red brick walls, hidden by overgrown horse chestnut branches that drooped over the sombre dark building. Once the doorbell sounded, immediate footsteps stomping heavily came ever closer towards us.

As the ancient door slowly creaked open, we were faced with frightening, scowling, shadowy figures that appeared at the front entrance, beckoning us to come inside. Obviously, they were expecting us, by the look on their faces, most probably thinking, heavens above…not more waifs and strays for us to look after!

I recall dad reassuring us, gently making hushing comforting noises, as he wiped our tears away with his white cotton handkerchief. He whispered through his own tear-filled eyes that we would be alright. As he said goodbye with a bird kiss on the cheek of my sister and me, he promised he would be back soon, that this would only be a short stay away from him, only for a while, until he could get us out again. He had to go through this same awful encounter and enactment as he left our two brothers at Nazareth Lodge for boys on the back road behind Nazareth House for girls, further down from where we were situated.

Tears and screams from my sister and I echoed as we were being snatched from our father's hands. Nuns in their veiled long black robes right down to their black leather shoes, harshly shoved us down a dimly sombre lit hallway into darkness and despair. This would become eight years of torment.

The nuns took my sister away from me. I was taken to the nursery, and my sister to a section on the other side of the building. We didn't see each other again for quite a while or until my dad, on rare occasions, could manage to visit us or take us out for the day or a weekend.

The clang of metal closing, and the grilles slamming tightly shut, before the main dark brown door was closed heavily with bolts in place. That was us, imprisoned, locked within four walls. We stepped into the sound of silence and a chamber-like hallway which led to what they called the parlour. From their well-presented, all-for-show area, the smell and intense aroma of arum lilies rose from the vases sitting beneath the statues of all the saints known to the Catholic Church. This part of the building, which was dressed up beautifully, was only a superficial entrance, evidently for important visitors, wealthy benefactors and, of course, the clergy.

As we entered a long and chilling cold, stoned paved tunnel area, this was when I was separated from my sister, in an act of finality. The nuns roughly snatched her away as we screamed in desperation and bewilderment, crying after each other. Then, the noise of heavy iron keys that securely locked the doors behind me reminded me that I was far away from my family home and normal family life and now from my sister and brothers. I found I was left alone.

Attempting to recall more of my earliest memories after being pulled apart from my sister midway in the gloomy hallway brings me back to the nursery where I was placed with other youngsters aged between two to five years old, all girls. Metal cots with bars were placed in rows; walls painted half magnolia and half pale, sickly shade of green. These colours made the building look and feel even colder than it was already, with old-fashioned iron radiators always cold and rusty grey, which gave out the images of a dungeon deep below the bowels of the ancient convent.

Children lying in cots crying loudly is my earliest memory, much of the crying probably being done by myself—wails of motherless and fatherless children crying out for comfort, reassurance and often with hunger. Too many children for the one nun to attend to when she religiously had to have her prayers said on bended knees four or more times a day. This practice took her away to the built-in chapel on the other side of the large building on its upper floors.

It wasn't too long after I'd been incarcerated into their care that any clothes and other items of my private personal property, which had been bought especially for me by my dad, were stolen from me in the middle of the night, stripping me of all my identity. I so vividly remember my bright, beautiful yellow jumper, which I loved and was so very proud of. It had a brown teddy bear emblazoned on the front of it and had drawn much attention from other children. I had worn it into Nazareth House but found it had disappeared. This broke my heart, knowing it was mine, a memory, and someone took it away from me. I kept searching around the dormitory for it, so clear is that memory to this day.

On outings, my dad took photographs of my family together, two boys and two girls standing by the embankment, by the Lagan river, or photos of us on Cave Hill, with the Napoleon's Nose Mountains in the background. He gave us these photographs as keepsakes to remind us that we belonged once to a family unit. But the religious orders, of course, frowned upon these acts of family togetherness and any signs of unity. Separation was their agenda and trademark. So many items were taken from me; Christmas presents given by Santa disappeared overnight also. Most probably, these were taken from me only to be rewrapped for the following Christmas if not deliberately removed as a cruel punishment. Yes, this same scenario happened to our colleagues in the South of Ireland and beyond in religious orders run institutions.

Unending was the humiliation of making children stand out in a line, with our underwear turned inside out, to be inspected by the nuns. It was seriously degrading and damaging to us. Children living in fear, only out of their nappies, yet they were warned to keep their pants clean. This is hard to believe, though it is so very true. This demeaning of children was still being carried out in the older girl's dormitory until the day I left and long after that! I was so terrified of being called out and being embarrassed by the nuns that I inadvertently hid my underwear underneath another cot on the other side of the room. I was not old enough to be aware that my name tag was sewn onto them. I remember to this day, as a very young child in the nursery, being told off, shouted at and made to feel so ashamed. We all lived with this distress and degrees of inhumane treatment throughout our time in institutional care.

At many of the nuns' prayer times, little girls from the 'grown-ups' dormitory would have been sent to the Babies section to babysit. These girls aged from ten to fourteen, who had been given no care in their many years in the nursery, were now being sent to look after little children no older than babies. They probably treated the infants as their toy dolls; most likely, they acted out the role of them being the mothers to the children, giving more attention to the youngsters than they would have had themselves. Oblivious to what was needed of them as babysitters, they, every one of them, desperately craved and needed the same tenderness and attention that had been denied to them all over the years. The normal, natural, caring, and nurturing that should have been present in this institution was non-existent in this place, unfortunately.

It was a massive change for the toddlers, from seeing no one in the babies' dormitory to seeing other girls who could well have been and often were, related to older family members sent to babysit their own siblings and doing so unknowingly.

The separation of siblings was a massive form of abuse inflicted upon children. It was kept hidden from children. Any form of relationship was not allowed for either sibling for fear of forming any kind of bond. Love and signs of affection were taboo subjects. Demonstrable love was absent, not shown amongst anyone, especially from the nuns themselves towards children who would have needed this the most.

From day one of being put through the ancient doors of this 'dungeon', it only instilled fear in me, a fear which grew into suspicion and eventually to a hatred of all those around me. This is what these institutions were fundamentally about; an indoctrination into mistrust, envy, hatred, violence, wrongdoings, and sin!

This treatment was the total opposite of what these institutions should have been all about and what they initially portrayed themselves outwardly to be. To the world outside, they were loving, kind, sympathetic, holy, pious, hardworking, and innocent godly creatures, though behind closed doors many of the nuns turned into anything but that.

The cruelty and continuing separation of siblings is still remembered by myself and my older sister. After hearing me crying for her behind the railings in the outer forecourts area, which separated us both, my sister often reached out to me with her hand to hold mine, but she and I were roughly pulled apart by the nun in charge, who always prevented any sign of love or care being shown.

Growing up in the nursery was not a pleasant, suitable or nurturing place to be in and should not ever have been allowed to operate as a place of sanctuary for young babies and toddlers. Because of the lack of care workers or outside help, having one nun on duty was quite obviously going to cause severe neglect and negligence to many children. Babies left to cry in soiled and wet nappies, unwashed, unfed, and unattended to. This scarred many children with severe mental health issues and deep complex needs, even before they were sent to the older girls' dormitories at the age of five. From the very beginning of my time in Nazareth House, I began to wet the bed. I was clearly distraught and distressed by being in a strange place away from my parents and siblings.

When I feel life is becoming so overwhelming, as memories of the past arise, I allow my memory to slip back into protective mode. This mode I have used on many occasions in Nazareth, and now, still many years later, even in my sixties, I tend to think back to times more soothing and uplifting and pleasant.

I think back in time to my wee granny, my father's mother, who was a homely granny who baked on her stove the most wonderful, delicious soda bread, rhubarb and apple tarts. The smell of granny's homemade cooking, her vegetable chicken soup made fresh in her little three-bedroom one-storey cottage, was Michelin star food compared to what we had force fed to us in Nazareth. Her little traditionally painted cottage with country blue window frames and brilliant white pebble-dashed front and gables walls, deep in the green fields of the countryside, stirred up a hunger inside of me for those early days of life and the natural and simple way of living.

Granny, as most of her neighbours did in those times, grew her own potatoes, vegetables, raised poultry and whatever she could afford to have on her little holding in order to survive. She had beautifully scented rose bushes, honey suckles, nasturtiums and all kinds of brightly coloured flowers at the back of the cottage, all round the sides and leading into her front garden, which ran along to the road in front.

The road outside the hedging of the cottage led to the church and graveyards and to the fast-flowing river filled with many rainbow trout, which professional fishermen longed to see and, above all, catch. Ah, but we children, my brother Kevin and I, with a willow branch, a piece of string borrowed from granny's potato crop, a hook found lying on the riverbank, we were able to cast off and catch the biggest of sought-after fish - a rainbow trout, to the envy of the experienced fishermen beside us on the bank. We screamed in panic as the fish took hold, not knowing what to do. A friendly fisherman came along, unhooked it, and did what needed to be done before handing it over to us with a smile, telling us how lucky we had been. What a memory! Granny was delighted to get the fish for dinner but not at the thought of us down by the river again, as she worried about us so much as we were supposed to be with our older siblings. Freedom!

Whilst in Nazareth House, my father came to visit us whenever he could, or when he was allowed to, at times taking us back out to the former family home in the early days, as he had promised before he had to give the family house up due to financial and health issues. Because of this and other problems, dad suffered a breakdown of sorts, causing large gaps in the time he saw us. Although he tried his best to visit whenever possible, he was often refused a visit with us, depending on which nuns were on duty. Sometimes, a decent nun from the old people's block allowed him into the hallway or corridor outside the classrooms, where he would always have goodies, sweets, biscuits, a toy or new socks or coats for us. At times on hearing from others that my dad was visiting and at the door, this nun who was also my teacher sister F, visibly tormented me with a smirk and a mockingly wry grin on her face. She always relished the fact that she would get a reaction from me, seeing me cry in anxiety and desperation, with her refusing the visit and telling the messenger to close the door and leave. When he was refused permission to come in, my dad used to stand up on a wall beside the Holy Rosary chapel next door to Nazareth and throw in sweets and oranges for us, determined that we would not be deprived of his kindness and assurance that he still cared for us.

When the school term ended, and on some holiday periods, he would always bring us back to my granny's cottage in the country, near the shores of Lough Neagh. She hadn't many material things, but we had freedom, happiness, love, and a protective covering over and around us. We played in the fields, making caves in the haystacks, roasting the potatoes straight from

17

the field, into an open fire made for us outdoors by dad or granny or our uncle. We made picnics of berries and sorrel leaves. We had makeshift tents, and my father's old cars in the field made magical memories for us. We pretended to drive away with my elder brother at the wheel, making revving noises and taking us on an imaginary journey. And, of course, our kittens were always with us on our laps. Even a chicken or two decided to jump on board. Our wee 'banty' hen, who was rejected and underweight, whom granny adopted and looked after as one of her own children, always followed us.

My Easter holidays memories were of the little new-born yellow baby chicks following the mother hen around the fields and at night helping granny round them up before they followed the mother hen into the chicken shed especially erected for breeding hens and their chicks. Placed safely away so no harm would come to them from the foxes that came out in the dark of night, assured they were fully protected, fed, mothered and safe, granny put the iron bars leaning heavily against the shutter boarding for extra security. Secure and away from the hands of marauding beasts in the darkness of the night. This protective act of kindness and security upon the chicks was breathtakingly beautiful and so special to see.

How lucky these chicks were to have the loving protection and a caring guardian over them, something we children certainly did not have in Nazareth. Oh, they were the happiest times of my life, just to get away from Nazareth.

It was heart-breaking when it was time to go back there, crying, screaming and wailing so much. The boys would beg my father to bring us girls back first and vice versa, so we could stay away a little longer. Then it was time to go through the wooden door and metal grilles, shoved down through the long dark hallway that went on forever, deep into darkness and despair once again.

What made it worse for us was we knew of the outside world and freedom, but this was snatched away from us every time we got back to the institution, our happiness becoming no more than a memory. Having to return from outings and return to Nazareth damaged us much more, I believe, than if we hadn't known the freedom, kindness, happiness and joy that decent human beings could bring us on the outside. A far cry from the traumatic experiences that went on within the walls of Nazareth.

What was about to happen in the very near future, as I moved over to the older girl's dormitory, was even more torturous, inhumane and absolutely life-changing...for all the wrong reasons. The next chapter of my journey into Hell was about to begin for real!

CHAPTER TWO

Where did my time in the infant's wing of Nazareth House go? I am trying to remember the actual move from the Nursery to the older girl's dormitory and exactly what age I was, aged five or nearing age six, perhaps? This timely transition and move coincided with the start of my regular primary school classes. I recall being in the same classroom as my sister for a short time, even though she was four years older than me. I still remember her art, the paintings she had drawn, and my amazement at how pretty the colours were that jumped from the pages and pictures she had illustrated. These brightened up the whole classroom as her colourful paint made them come to life. Strangely, I hadn't seen or noticed these bright and beautiful colours in my surroundings during my time in the Nursery. Colour had been erased from my mind and my vision, most likely because of the drab and colourless walls which surrounded me in time spent in the younger children's section of Nazareth.

From my early years on entering Nazareth, dark browns and blacks had instilled a fear in me, ominous cycles of doom and gloom. All these newly rainbow colours and shades of land and sea, even on paper, made me feel alive, happier and hopeful once again, even if only for a short time. This joy would soon fade as I was taken away from these moments of tranquillity in my sister's classroom and back into the reality of the harsh, colourless dungeon-like building I was now in.

I felt I'd recently been wrapped in cold storage for a few years in the Nursery, as now I had recently thrown off the baby clothing, just as a baby caterpillar growing up changes into a cocoon-like entity. It learns in the changeover to shed its old skin, strengthen itself in the process, develop into its potential, live, and be ready for the next stage in moving forward.

I had just stepped into a brand-new realm, now walking and no longer crawling from one darkened tunnel into another. I was not there yet, but somehow, this was a process I had to endure to survive, a sequencing of my development cycles taking place, letting nature take its course. Now though, this one led me through to believing, somehow, I would see an end to the darkness and that I was being led closer to the end of this tunnel and eventually onwards to brighter times ahead, one day perhaps! One day, indeed, a beautiful pretty butterfly would develop, colourful and bright, no longer dull and drab, but precious and valued coming out of the chaos of storms and struggles.

Now I was moving on, a little bit older, and more aware that I had survived coming through the early first stages of life in care and was now prepared, even if a little, to step into the next phase and once again to whatever lay beyond that. Always on the move from one season to the next, in trepidation and fearful anticipation.

Being back together again with my sister in the same part of the building was only for a few years or less, as my sister moved out to live with our father soon after. I only recall very few instances of her being around, and at those times when she was, I felt at ease knowing her bed, at least, was in the same room. This was before the nuns in charge separated us again and moved my bed to the other side of the dormitory, which was part of their regular uncaring routine.

I wonder often just how they came to be this way. I'm sure they couldn't have always been like this. (I have recently watched a programme called "The Stanford Prison Experiment", whereby to many, the Stanford experiment underscored those findings, revealing the ease with which regular people, if given too much power, could transform into ruthless oppressors).

And so, we ask, why treat young children so harshly, so cruelly? Did being locked up behind the four walls affect them, too, just as it did us? Was this behaviour passed down from one set of nuns in charge to others as they entered the convent? What possessed them? Did they allow the devil himself to take over their senses by believing they were doing well if they prayed useless, meaningless prayers? Even the devil himself, would know they were falling right into his trap and were on their way to the Hell that they often told us little ones, was the place that we were heading to. Did they not realise that their behaviour towards vulnerable children would forfeit their chances of ever getting to their mansion place in heaven?

They believed they were doing God's work by beating the sin out of us. We, in their eyes, were the unholy spawn of the devil. The tears that flowed daily from the children were collected and carried by their God to remind Him of the sins they, the nuns themselves, committed and not of the little children. One day He would punish them for the torment, pain and suffering that was meted out upon the apples of His eye. Genuine Christian servants would have known that God watches over and protects the most vulnerable.

Only in the shadow of my sister's watchful eye did I ever feel safe, even though she, too, came under attack. Seeing this happen to your own sister or family member or friends was painful, even more so than the attacks upon myself at times. This carried on with no protection for either of us. Unfortunately, and so sadly, some of the older girls would turn into bullies and would attack any of the younger children, just as they, too, had been attacked when they were younger. It was all they ever knew, this being a continuous cruel, vicious cycle over and over, year in and year out! Power, without the overseeing of safeguarding policies, or disciplinary procedures, ran rampant and out of control, all behind closed doors and high walls, with no one asking questions or caring to do so.

We were often and always used as 'enslaved' children to do things for the older girls also, as well as the nuns, fetching items for them or doing whatever they decided was needed of us. We were too terrified not to do what they wanted, knowing this would lead to yet more beatings. Many children had come into the care system from abusive family settings, so it was obvious that what they went through outside would be discussed or acted out amongst others in care. Listening to or being around some of those stories was uncomfortable, sickening, and disturbing, especially if those so young did not know anything about the nature of which they spoke.

Children talked about things I'd never known anything about. They used certain words and language to describe specific incidents. Descriptive nuances I did not want to hear of, even in my ever so young and immature mind. I knew, somehow, it sounded horrendous and revolting. I tried to escape being around some of these older girls, not knowing what they must have suffered before coming into the Homes. It was apparent now that they were crying out to tell someone what they had gone through. (Was this in preparation for my future, one wonders!) Why tell me?

Though, what stays in my mind is being summoned to stand behind the chairs and pick stuff out of the older girl's hair, likened to apes and monkeys in the jungle, picking out dandruff, nits, or 'crawly creepers' as we called them.

This all happened whilst the older girls watched TV and as a nun half dozed in a corner, laying back on an old rocking chair but still reading, her glasses noticeably falling off the tip of her nose. She owned an old smelly black Mynah bird with a yellow beak called Bobby, and it got fed grapes and decent fruit, which we children did not. The nun brought these up to her decent quarters next to the parlour area after dinner. He, the Mynah, was so noisy and dirty. His cage was smelly, with droppings all over the table and floor, and we had to clean up after it. If we did not, we would be shoved around and roughed up by the big girls to make sure we did what was ordered of us, if the nun wasn't around.

This room was on the middle floor of the high-up, sizeable three-storey building. Each floor was named after a saint, and we were assigned to that group name. St. Anne's was where my sister was placed on her admission to Nazareth House, just after we had been pulled apart and was now where I had recently been allocated after a few years away from her.

23

This chair-filled room with an old black and white television, high up on a wall, was always filled up on a Saturday, one of the main days when all us girls of all ages had gotten together. Saturday afternoon was always a time for watching Dr Who and the Daleks, the dark, frightening music of scientific 'out of this world' events, with a weird-sounding drone that haunts me still. More so, it heightened the effect that I was living inside a bubble or an outer space-like planet that was not on this earth nor belonged within it. This place had its own rules and regulations apart from the outside world, and all were free to lay down the law, to punish and harshly discipline, unchallenged and unhindered.

We were allowed back into the dormitory next door at bedtime, where we slept in rows of iron beds, with a large wrought iron long pipe running along the back of our beds. This pipe which was supposed to be turned on in winter and cold evenings and nights, was rarely warm. I recall having to attempt drying my socks and underwear on this pipe, as many of us did after washing them out before the nun saw them soiled. We put them inside our horsehair-filled pillows or between the sheet and the horsehair-stripped mattress when they did not dry. We hoped the heat from our little bodies would dry our clothes for us.

Curtainless windows in the dormitories are a frightening memory to look back on as storms raged in the night, with heavy thunder almost lifting us out of our beds and the blinding flashes of lightning which terrifyingly lit up the once-darkened rooms. The older girls would shout, "It's the end of the world!" as we screamed out in fear. We were often told that God's wrath was coming upon us because of our sins. It made us believe that we were now finally in Hell. Scare stories and rumours usually spread around the Institution that Our Lady had told the nuns that the end was soon. Apparently, this was revealed in secret conversations with whom she appeared. Also, rumours that if anyone's second name began with the letter O, they were first to die and stories that a Third World War was about to start where nuclear bombs would fall on us, and we would all die. Non-stop horror tales and ghost stories of banshees and headless saints that roamed the bedrooms at night caused us even more terrifying nightmares made worse by no comfort, protection or reassurance that they were only tall tales.

The large plain see-through glass couldn't, and wouldn't ever, cover up the darkness of the night. Therefore, it frightened us all the more. We could see the dark shadows and the movement of tall tree branches swaying around wildly by the stormy winds. Even though this wild spectacle of the night was on the outside, the eerie goings-on seemed ever so close to us, believing inwardly that the many loose branches were reaching into the darkened room towards our beds. The large dormitory was sectioned off by a long broad, curtain-like partition, separating us into smaller groupings, yet we could still hear and see others if we peeped around them. This enabled us all to listen to the latest gossip, which was exciting, though when we heard them telling scary stories, we often tried to cover our ears and hide under the sheets and counterpane that surrounded them.

As a result of living in fear and the threat of bad beatings, my constant bed-wetting continued. This is a recognised medical condition and one of severe distress and separation anxiety. Because of this, I was punished even more by the nuns. This included being forced to sit on a potty in front of all the other girls in the middle of the night, just as other girls were made to. Everyone would be made to watch our ordeal. Other times we were left to lie in wet, urine, soaked beds.

In due course, the nuns introduced a very unusual and cruel contraption for the bed-wetters. A heavy brown rubber tarpaulin-like mackintosh with electric currents attached was used to shock us children in our sleep whenever urine touched the live wires attached to the rubber cover beneath our sheets. This electric shock treatment would jolt us awake with a buzzing noise linked into the nun's cell-like room at the end of the dormitory. This was not in the '30s or '40s but in the mid/late 1960s. Why was this allowed? Indeed, it was illegal, or was it? But who was to know or find out? It was only us the unwanted rejects, hidden behind four walls, deep within the unholy dwellings of an ancient dungeon.

When it was discovered that any of us had wet the bed again, we were thrown into a bath with 'Jeyes fluid', a powerful lethal disinfectant, with a warning stating, 'not to be used on humans, for sewage and drainpipes only'. This disinfectant was poured into bath water that was constantly cold, into which we were dipped in and out, just like sheep are in a farmyard, this after being scrubbed harshly with a scrubbing brush. This horrendous ordeal was carried out upon children as a punishment, warning us not to wet the bed again. Of course, it was counterproductive as we returned straight to the cold baths.

During this punishment, we had to endure emotional abuse from the nuns. They would shout at us, calling us 'disgusting', 'smelly', 'filthy', and much worse. Crying out for them to stop did not deter them, and they seemed to enjoy going into a mad rage and using a strap and whatever else was at hand to thrash us. They who laid down the rules and how they treated us resulted in the children mimicking and acting out what they saw in terms of how their superiors, the nuns, acted in front of them.

Eventually, we began to believe what was happening was our fault and that the nuns were always right. We thought that we were the bad children, unwanted children. A few inspections were carried out in later years, and we were given specific orders. We were warned not to speak, told to smile, look happy, and directed to clean the dormitories, classrooms, and sitting rooms, all in preparation to make it look like we were in a perfectly loving family care home.

Slave labour was the order of the day for the nuns and was an everyday occurrence, and was, of course, always on the top of their agenda. They believed we should work hard for a living. We would not be 'kept', as it were...for nothing in return. This meant we had to be on our knees as we scrubbed their Institution clean from top to bottom whilst praying for forgiveness for our unworthy sinful souls. This is what we *deserved* as sinners and mere mortals.

As soon as we got bellowed at to get out of bed early in the mornings, if we didn't jump out quick enough, on the sound of loud clanging bell, we were commanded to our knees in prayer. Then after a cold wash, we had a breakfast of the same inedible food. Most children preferred our evening meal, the bread and jam, though not with the horrible sour and smelly Stork margarine. Then it was scrubbing and cleaning time for some, for those girls who were unlucky enough to be pulled out of breakfast to do this. Then, others got called out of classes as we went to our classrooms, some to clean up and to do chores if the nuns decided they were not good enough to bother being taught. They marked children out by placing dunce caps made of paper on our heads and putting us in a corner, shaming and humiliating us on every occasion they could.

Saturdays and mid-weekly chores were us youngsters on our knees, either praying or scrubbing wooden corridor floors, then polishing them until they shone brightly. I only recall a few employed cleaners being brought in, mainly in the kitchens washing the pots and greasy cooking trays. We also did the yearly spring cleaning, climbing onto tables to reach the windows and magnolia-painted walls, which we washed down with a squeezy yellow sponge attached to a long pole. A thick orange wax in large tins got embedded in our eyes, nails and hair every time we clawed it out with small grey rags, the polish plopping everywhere around us. We spent hours doing this, often without a drink of water or food, as the work had to be finished before mealtimes.

Whenever the nuns did disappear at times, we would make slides up and down the shiny floors falling all over on top of each other, a momentary lapse of the law and us having fun. It was a necessity to have us working for a living, anything at all to make use of us children, with nuns standing guard over us, not allowing us to speak to each other, or worse still, not to dare laugh.

We didn't have much fun, though we got to play skipping games in the forecourt, with a large rope and hopscotch. During those times, we felt free to play just as typical children on the outside would have done and to enjoy ourselves, even for a while.

I remember having a few new toys or games hidden inside my clothes that I'd brought back from family outings. The girls were always delighted to see new inventions, mainly as many did not get outside often, so this was always a lovely surprise for them. I had long learned never to show the nuns anything I had brought back, lest they be confiscated once again.

As was a usual punishment theme, my being thrown outside in the bare empty courtyard, I would jump on one of only two working rusty swings.

I would manoeuvre the swing to go higher than high to wave frantically at passers-by, or to catch a glimpse of the double-decker buses driving by, with normal people on them, hoping somehow they could see me. I often shouted out to them, whether literally or in my being, begging them to get me out. I always wanted to escape from the clutches of the nuns and was determined one day I would! I heaved up so high to look over the tops of the heavily barbed wire red-bricked walls, if only to see the big world outside.

Because the nuns were away a lot praying, I would often sneak away from whoever was supposed to watch over us, and those mainly children only a few years older than us. I recall roaming around in my early years, trying to break out of the building to get away from it, the memory so vivid in my mind. An older girl was sent to get me back and ran down the inside walls towards a gateway after me. I ran away at a very early age, even then. Now placed in the section for older girls further across the same building, with the older people's block situated in between, I still managed to escape by climbing through railings or slipping through open corridor doors to reach the outer gardens, mainly towards the front of Nazareth.

I never got too far as the gates and wooden doors were always tightly shut, with metal grilles over them. The walls were far too high for a child to climb over. Outside the older people's department, which was situated close by, I found handbags that old ladies had thrown from windows, powder puffs, makeup pouches, lipsticks, and stale smelling perfumes. I often picked up tablets lying loose below the outside windows. I still remember the smell and taste of the tablets. I had put them into my mouth hungrily, thinking these tablets were sweeties and only spitting them back out again when they made me feel sick—a big disappointment to a young child, as they looked inviting with such attractive colours. I recall the taste in my mouth still as I think back. God must have saved my life long back then too.

Whilst often left alone outside in the courtyard, I was forced to spend hours trying to amuse myself by playing with the spiders on the walls and counting worms in the patchy grassless lawn. In the otherwise lifeless uninhabitable playground with nothing in it, only a rusty couple of metal bars and two rusty and mainly broken swings that left our bodies, legs and arms covered in brown rust marks. The so-called playground or forecourt was a cold and lonely place, with only the cries of children echoing through the walls coming from the dormitories. These sorrowful wails mingled with the screeching of large black ravens and black and white magpies hovering from the trees and rooftops and within the darkened eaves of the chapels on either side of the yard. Menacing birds of prey looking down upon us, intimidating, and threatening, so not unlike the nun's manner and attitude, with the same black and white attire they wore as one entity. Hearing the peal of the chapel bells ring out on the hour is yet another torturous memory, with the bells of The Angelus at noon and six o'clock in the evenings always on time, never-ending triggers of religious ceremonies without the evidence of any form of Christlike behaviour attached. Meaningless!

We were always forced to put on poorly fitted shoes of the wrong size, often squeezing our feet into smaller-sized shoes that had been passed down so many times to others throughout the years. This affected so many of the girl's feet, including my own and my sister's, leaving us with lifelong bone defects of, bunions and problems relating to the natural growth of our feet. We had to wear flimsy light second-hand hand me down clothes, such as ragged short dresses with no sleeves, ankle socks or none in winter. We were lucky if we had a cardigan. If it had gone missing, we did without. In late autumn and winter, we did not have adequate clothing for the time of year and were still left outside daily in the cold. This happened to me in rain, hail or snow, and I was left there until I was permitted to return.

I could be left outside for hours some days. When we were out on the forecourt, I often tried to get back in, but the older girls would push me and others back outside under the guidance of whatever nun was on duty. I remember being so cold I was frozen to the core. I often could not feel my hands or feet, and my face would be blazing red from the harshness of the elements. Many of these times, I would have walked over to the railings hoping I could see or hear from someone, perhaps a messenger from my family had called to pick me up, to take me away from this loveless place. The yearning, praying and built-up hope waiting for my miracle to happen was only to be dampened by the heavy footsteps of someone shouting, telling me it was time to go back inside.

If only I became very sick, I could be free to be discharged to the hospital for the day. Though it was a rarity for the nuns to take anyone to the hospital, their medicine was brown iodine slapped onto any injury, stinging open wounds, agonisingly burning until we were on fire and in more pain. The only doctor brought in was a Dr Hunter, and that was on infrequent occasions. All injuries were hidden behind those four walls so that no one would find out, or so they thought! And no one dared to ask, and if they did, the nuns made up one excuse after another, permanently preventing the truth from emerging into the public domain.

I had overheard some of the girls saying that they had gotten outside the walls of the Institution to go to the dentist, albeit legitimately, as they were allowed to go and were escorted there and back. I then claimed I, too, had a toothache. I got out to see a dentist, where he almost suffocated me with gas, using a brown rubber thick heavy nose bag forced over my nose and mouth until I was completely knocked out. The dentist carried on and removed what seemed to me to be an excellent tooth. Indeed, he should have known this as my teeth were always good, but no, he pulled it out, and after he did so, I was sent back to Nazareth. There I was, left to lie in my vomit, crying out for help in the bottom dungeon room, away from anyone. Once again, there was no one around who cared.

No one came to my aid for the remainder of that day, and I thought I was dying. I thought my time was finally up, and I would no longer be a part of this horrible world that only ever harmed me and was never good. Finally, I came round, and only after many hours lying in a foetal position was I allowed upstairs, still faint, exhausted and sickened of dentists forever.

The bullying and abuse continued on holidays and holy days! There were a few trips away in the summertime, and yes, it was good to get away from the dark dungeons of Nazareth, but why do I choose not to remember all those times if they were supposed to be happy? If we did not get out with my father or to my granny's house, we had to go along with the nuns who brought us away to Co. Down or the Glens of Antrim. I do not have good memories of these places; they were old army billets with doors and railings painted dark brown and grey exteriors and interiors. This building in Glenarriff was set deep among the forested area and again had dark, brown old frightening stairways, halls, and basements.

If only Nazareth and other institutions had been safe and secure places to have children placed into, the people in charge could have, would have, checked up on children during their times away from 'care'! Whether on summer holidays or weekend breaks, if only to check we were exactly where we should have been, with the right people, and that the families who took the young girls away for weeks were vetted and were at least reliable and trustworthy. The nuns and government should have had strict rules in place and a reassurance that the children would be safe, but more so, that the children were sensitively questioned about their time away on return to care homes. If spoken to gently and in a kind and caring manner about their breaks, but more importantly, believed if they stated anything untoward had happened to them whilst away from them, it would have been a better approach. Sadly, this never happened.

This is what it was like growing up in Nazareth. We were made to feel ashamed of anything to do with the human body. The nuns had told us everything about our bodies was sinful: to hide our nakedness, to keep our hands closed under our chins, as in prayer when we slept, or to place them across our chest. I was never able to understand why.

I did not know the ways of the world outside, as we had not been taught nor warned of how or why we should keep girls' bodies safe from marauding men or women and what the difference was in various types of abuse. Indeed, what was abuse?

Many people from the neighbouring parish chapel next door and other parishes throughout the North called at holiday times, offering to take children to their family homes and farms. I am sure many of these holidays away were first class, and the children were well looked after, though, unfortunately, I know many of them that were not. Why, if the nuns were showing children what way to sleep at night, were they not concerned about their whereabouts whilst outside on trips away? Why did no one check up on them or ask questions when the girls arrived back? Did anyone care, really care? No, very few ever did.

I know first-hand when many of the children told the nuns that they were assaulted, whether it be sexually or physically, by those who took them out on breaks, that the nuns would not believe them, instead punishing the children, for ever to dare accuse these decent church-going people of such things, or to even speak of these ungodly acts! If ever at all, these torrid unimaginable incidents took place, always assuming the children were telling lies. Children were never believed, hence the fear of daring to tell the nuns we had been assaulted on holiday in the first place. They cared more about this news getting out to the congregations. 'Why, goodness gracious, they would never, ever donate money or leave their wills to support the religious holy orders! And that would never do!' The self-preservation of the church and the religious orders came first at all costs!

Throughout my time at Nazareth, I endured acts of physical violence by various nuns. After a beating, one of many by Sister F, I realised I had a lot of bad bruising on my arms, though this was normal to me, and I took no notice of it as I was always covered in bruising or cuts, but someone whom I thought didn't care about me anymore did notice—my dad.

One time when I was allowed out for a day, my father questioned me about what had happened to my arms which he had noticed were covered in dark bruising. I explained that on this occasion, it was only Sister F, as she often did, had grabbed me by my arm and dragged me after her, swinging me around by the arms and throwing me about like a rag doll. When my dad was leaving me back, he asked to see one of the nuns to get an explanation as to what had happened to me. After my father left, I suffered an even more violent attack from Sister F. Her nickname was Elephant, because of her loud and thunderous footsteps, letting us know she was back on the warpath. She beat me with a large bamboo stick while calling me a liar and evil and said I was the worst type of person to have entered her holy and precious convent. When she had finished her attack, she locked me in a dark cupboard, and I lay there in the dark for many hours, alone, crying in pain and wishing again I were dead.

32

This complaint against them from my dad, which they denied, only made them more abusive. I never again dared to tell anyone whenever I got beaten up by them, knowing it only got me into worse trouble. I somehow got used to and expected the assaults just as I did from the notorious Sister K, who was a very rough and tough nun. We called her bulldog as she would roar loudly at the children, often grabbing me violently by the hair and pulling my ears. She would yank my hair so hard that lumps of it came out as I was dragged from her banister which we used as a slide, from the top floor to the second floor. These incidents were harrowing and occurred often, but it was a way of life inside Nazareth and something we had finally become accustomed to.

Often the nuns and their helpers on hair wash days, would pour almost boiling water over our heads from tin jugs as we were made to lean over a metal wash basin. Then they used a metal lice comb on our scalps to eliminate lice, even if our heads were clean. The pain of this torturous ritual was unbearable, and standing queuing up and waiting for our turn, made us shake, cry and tremble with trauma.

Incidents that traumatised me were when the nuns cut my hair and that of other children. They held these gigantic black rusty scissors in front of us as they deliberately cut children's lovely long hair, or those with beautiful curly locks, removing our hair close to the scalp almost hacking of our ears as they did so. They hacked at it crudely after putting us into a chair, often in the open forecourt, in the playground, knowing the other children would be there. This was another form of punishment.

This dehumanisation and blatant torture of children left us in a state of irreparable instability, halting a natural, normal growth cycle. Living through this abuse led us to suffer many ailments and other severe issues. This was also to be detrimental to our fitting in with society. It affected our potential to stay in lasting employment, our ability to form relationships and our capability to trust anyone. Worse to come was how to learn to create a loving, everlasting bond with our siblings, if ever this was possible and, in the future, how to know how to express love or display emotions to our children, because of what many went through in our most formative years.

The corporal punishments they used on us ranged from slaps with thick leather straps beneath our clothes on our thighs, making red welts and burning blistered markings that hurt so much we could not sit or sleep. Large bunches of keys were often used to hit us over the head, or backs, whilst being dragged into a cupboard like a storeroom and left for hours and hours in the dark, not given any food or even allowed to go to the toilet.

Mealtimes were held in a drab dank room called the refectory. This was also a difficult and traumatic experience. We had to say grace before all meals and line up to a hatch for our food, not allowed to sit down until we were told to. The food was always of poor quality, with inedible waste innards of animals which the nuns could get without paying for. We were fed old decaying vegetables that farmers donated, surpluses they couldn't sell themselves. We got the leftovers unfit for their customers, but sure, it was alright for us orphans to eat. No one would ask questions if we got food poisoning which I'm sure we did on many occasions, leaving us violently sick. The milk we were given was often sour, and the apples I would search for out of sheer hunger had worms, making me sick again. The farmers left their unwanted produce in, and the nuns gave them all the scraps of food, which were thrown into old greasy buckets in the depths of the building at the back of the kitchens.

Yet hungry as we were, we still were forced to eat everything tasteless and inedible they served us. If it was meat, it was dressed as a sausage but mostly it was tough gristle, making me choke constantly. I was sickened terribly by this and the rotten eggs, which were black and blue, not yellow, and after I was sick, they would spoon-feed me by force. I often vomited and gagged further because of this force-feeding. I remember witnessing many children being forced to eat this awful food. If we were not eating quickly enough, we were slapped around the head or ears and had our hair pulled, made to fall of our chairs as we cried in anguish. We were not allowed to leave the table until our plates were empty.

I had heard many speak of rummaging around in the buckets eating scraps meant for the pig farmer. Such was the hunger. Not knowing or caring it wasn't appropriate to do such a thing, we noticed the leftovers that were thrown into these buckets were food that we hadn't got served, jelly mixed with apple tart and melted ice cream, which tasted much nicer spilt over the jelly and sponge cake. I remember getting teased for years about being called 'Sponge Cake' because one of the priests was continuously fed sponge cake. This was one of the younger priests, whom we noticed the nuns would swoon over. The nuns and whoever was on duty often made threats to us. I was frequently told that I would never see my father, brothers, or sister again and would never be allowed out. This caused me great distress, and I often cried my heart out either in bed at night or sat on the old threadbare ancient chairs in the corner of the sitting room. Tears again fell in the playground with my face always turned into the walls, lest they dared see me crying, as it was frowned upon, and we got slapped and beaten if found to be doing so. Emotions of any kind were not to be shown or displayed. No wonder we had nightmares, screaming and crying in terror in our sleep, biting into the sheets to muffle out the sounds, and dreams of having our lives taken from us by those in black, faceless, hooded garments. Torturous!

When the nuns were not bullying us, they were on their knees in the chapel before the cross of Christ, praying empty hollow prayers that I am sure never reached heaven.

I do remember priests calling into the convent regularly. They had their specific sitting room or parlour in which they were served the best of food, such as sponge cakes and always with the finest China tea sets. I cannot remember at all for what reasons we would have been in the presence of the clergy. I know I have deliberately blocked so much out. We went to confession in front of the priests in the dark confessionals, in the dark wooden, cold, eerie-looking chapel above the fire escapes. We were under immense pressure to tell the priest our sins and wrongdoings. We had not a clue what sins we had committed, so we made them up and repeated the same tirade of repetitive confessions week in and out. I often wonder, did the nuns and priests ever confess their sins and wrongdoings to God? Perhaps they became so used to what they did that they became desensitised to their behaviour, believing they were in God's service, which was all in His Holy name.

Nobody's child, nobody wants me, I'm nobody's child, was a popular song the nuns got us children to sing in front of them and visiting priests and religious dignitaries as they sat in the hall eating the best of food and being attended to by the nuns who couldn't do enough for them. Nuns were fussing over them, with only the best silver teapots and cutlery.

How could they be so cold and insensitive to our despair? Our loss of parents and a family home, whilst demanding us to sing it out at the top of our voices that "I'm nobody's child, nobody wants me, I'm nobody's child, no mummy's kisses or no daddy's smile, nobody wants me, I'm nobody's child." The priests and nuns clapped as we were made to sing out those very words. Heartless, unfeeling and cruel! As well as singing, we had to put on shows for them, concerts, plays, dressing up and dancing. All this for the clergy, the well-heeled congregation, the neighbouring elite and, of course, the local public servants and their ilk to show what a wonderful time we children were having. This was all a colossal act, a performance, the nuns knowing that if the highly esteemed audience enjoyed the show, the collections of money and donations of goods and whatever else would be much higher and forthcoming, seeing what a good job the nuns were doing.

This when they, the nuns, went out collecting two by two, walking around with their begging bowls and made up feigned sad faces, bent down as beleaguered paupers...manipulating and persuading the already impoverished poor people of the districts to contribute to their life-giving cause. This is a renowned ploy. Whether right or wrong, the religious orders have often asked pensioners to think about donating or leaving the contents of their wills to the great work the charity was doing for the most vulnerable and unfortunate.

Up and down the land, there were collection boxes in every shop corner, every church, and every school, pleading for donations to help the orphans. The collection boxes were inside the orphanages too, but these were all for the black and white babies of Africa and foreign countries. Later we heard that all this money and the collections were allegedly going to...the headquarters in Hammersmith of the poor Sisters of Nazareth! We, the poor children, the orphans and the displaced children, got nothing! The clothes, toys, gifts and other donated items were sold off at their Jamborees held in country villages in rural areas to make more money for themselves and their headquarters in London. There is a photograph with us children gathered around a brand-new large slide, bought by a wealthy benefactor. He is standing behind us, with the nuns looking on, making us look happy. The giant slide wasn't ever seen again as soon as the gentleman left the building. It was most likely sold off to the highest bidders!

I can remember my father always giving my sister money for the nuns after we visited with him, and when my sister left the convent, he gave it to me to give to them. I can recall being asked by Sr. Kevin, 'Did my father not give them any money this week?' I, as a child, did not know what that was all about.

One day in late 1967, I was dismissively and bluntly told by a nun in the corridor who had come past me in a rush that I had to leave the convent and go back and live in the house that my father had recently acquired. Her attitude towards me as a young child only nearing eleven years of age, to delight in throwing me out of their convent, left me almost shell-shocked. For the first time in a long time, it now seemed that the typically robust and action-filled place surrounding me was in complete silence. It felt like no one was around, I could hear nothing but my breathing and my heart beating loudly. I was stunned into complete silence. I could not believe my ears; I was left alone. I was not brought to any office for a consultation or given my bus or taxi fare to travel the long journey. Immediately, I had to set in motion what I should do. How can I manage this, how do I leave, will they give me a suitcase with my belongings or anything I wondered to myself. For a young child, to walk a mile or two to the bottom of the road and not be offered any companionship for the long walk I was about to take that day was unimaginable. I was told to leave just the way I stood, with no suitcase, no belongings, no money, or no goodbyes.

This was a different form of rejection from being disowned by my mother, and I felt then by my father, my brothers and my sister. I had been alone with other home girls, as we were called, for so long and now even these people I'd grown up with did not want me it seemed like. What did I do wrong now? I know I always got the blame for everything anyway, but I had gotten used to that over the years. I began to inadvertently expect and await the guilt, beatings, and ostracisation. I had become accustomed to this; I was now programmed into an institutionalised robotic figure. This is what they transformed me into.

I was no longer that innocent, happy child, the little three-year-old. They had reprogrammed me, just as animals in cages in a laboratory are tested upon, leaving them subservient to their master's desires, being used and abused. They turned me into something, not of myself but of what they wanted me to be, to live under their control, submit to their commands, and obey like a robot would do in an inanimate manner, devoid of emotion and feeling. They stripped me of my identity and left me a shell of my former self. I was now under their control. They won. Now, I was being released from their clutches, their prison cells, as their job was done. I was just like an animal that had been used as part of an experiment for many years and was now of no use. I'd passed my sell-by date, and I was to be thrown out.

Why? Was it because my father stopped giving them money, perhaps not enough money? I knew at that time he was not working, and had my other siblings back with him again, although my two brothers would end up back in an institution shortly after. I still do not know why the nuns could be allowed to do this without welfare or social services being informed. I have yet to hear from anyone. I needed to prepare. I was just told to leave! It was a shock even though I longed to be free. I had been inside the orphanage for so long that I did not see myself ever getting to be completely set free. I, by that time, may have even consigned myself to the fact that I would never be free. I was bewildered, afraid and fearful even though I was now free to go, but to whom? I had not seen my siblings in quite a while or my dad, and because of the separation and length of time apart, our bonds had utterly broken, so I felt alone. I did not feel I was a part of a family anymore. The damage was already done. Mentally and psychologically, I was damaged goods.

It's medically factual that babies and young children who have been neglected and abused mentally, emotionally, physically, and worse, sexually, in their most formative years will carry the effects of this trauma and go on to

38

suffer from complex post-traumatic stress disorder into teenage years, adulthood and onwards into old age.

Before I walked out the back wooden gate, I dared to go into the sewing room to ask if I could have something to wear. They looked at me in disbelief as I told the much older workers...the nuns had me leaving the convent for good and I would not be coming back, but I had no clothes to wear! They begrudgingly, with a look on their faces which said, 'How dare you ask us for clothing!', threw me an old pink and white dress that I used to wear on outings. I felt so embarrassed, degraded, and belittled by how the much older girls treated me then. Even in my last few minutes of being in the orphanage of the Nazareth Convent, they sarcastically sneered and ridiculed me as I was leaving. Such was the manner and design of being raised in their care!

No one walked me to the gate as I left Nazareth. It was held open and slammed tightly shut as I hurried out to the main street behind the large building that had been my home for the past eight years. I was alone again, having to plan my long journey down to where my dad now lived with my other siblings. But now, I was fearful of how they would receive me. The rejection and torment I had come through all these years had taken hold of me mentally and emotionally. As I sidled along the high walls of the convent, I hugged myself tightly, squeezing my arms around me, hoping to make myself shrink or disappear. With my head bent and my face turned close to the wall, I walked as fast as possible. Now my dream was coming true. At long last, I was leaving that horrible building. I was free to go from my past life and into a future I knew nothing about, not knowing what lay there for me. Little did I know that my past life in Nazareth would never truly leave me alone. I would carry the stigma instilled within me into very late life. I felt like an outcast, a leper who wasn't allowed to be near anyone in society lest I spread some terrible disease upon them.

I walked through alleyways and clung closely to garden hedgerows hoping no one could notice my feelings of shame and embarrassment hanging heavily upon my shoulders. After all those years of torture, I felt I was carrying the weight of many insults, pain, suffering and rejection. I clasped tightly to my only possession, my pink and white checked dress. I had nothing else, as I allowed my hair to cover my face, hiding my shame, sin, and brokenness. I was labelled, marked out as an alien, and not of this beautiful world for beautiful people. How was I ever going to fit into it, I thought to myself in fear and trepidation.

I now had to plan for my survival, to protect myself against the outside world, unaware that this would again be another short chapter of my life. I walked the long road, finally getting to our front door. My dad seemed very surprised and shocked to see me standing there. I took that look like a sign of rejection. Already, I was perceiving and projecting how people looked at me or how they spoke to me as a sign of ridicule, or they didn't want me, or that I was troublesome and unwanted. He probably only was taken aback to see me, as the welfare or nuns didn't let him know I was getting out for good. Though I had become accustomed to feeling I wasn't wanted anywhere, I immediately felt the same right at this moment, landing on his doorstep. This was now the scene set for the rest of my life. I was emotionally and mentally broken. What I had to endure for all those years finally took its toll on me. The abuse I had received was now seeping through every pore of my being. Yes. I was damaged goods.

CHAPTER THREE

After I left that horrendous hellhole of a prison-like convent, I was unable to feel that I fitted into society or was ever going to be a part of it again. No matter how much I tried to integrate, it didn't help. Even after many long years of yearning to be a part of 'normal' society, I somehow knew I was different from others and would always be an outsider. Being removed from my family home and placed into the nursery in the care home, then years later to the older girl's domain, I once again had to prepare for another transition. What was always on my mind and in my thoughts were the words of the song I mentioned in the last chapter that they made us sing: *I'm nobody's child...no Mummy's kisses or no Daddy's smile...Nobody wants me...I'm nobody's child.*

I often wondered to myself, what did we ever do to deserve being the scapegoats of the nun's anger and rage?...Why were none of these people ever held to account? Were they never, ever worried nor concerned that any of the children might reveal to someone what was going on for decades inside of those ungodly buildings or that one day in the future, the police would be involved? Why not? Because they were a law unto themselves. Power and control had overtaken their senses, and these ungodly traits that had been ingrained within them over many, many years were now the false gods and ideologies they served religiously in order to prey dominance over innocent, vulnerable children. To them, we were nothing but a black stain, a mortal sin, a disgrace to society and to the holy church to which they allegedly prayed and bowed down to.

Crying out for help within myself, but never ever asking for it, made me fester in anger and rage and with no one to understand me, I took on another persona. I acted out as if I didn't care, pretended to be happy, and if anyone dared to question me about my previous whereabouts, I'd tell them I lived with my granny in the country. If they kept badgering me, I'd tell them to mind their own business and get angry to hopefully make them afraid to ever ask me questions again.

I soon got to learn and manage how to get people to leave me alone. I no longer was going to allow anyone to bully me, humiliate or torture me. I was now going to stand up for myself, and no one was going to get away with hurting me again if I could help it. I was now free. No longer locked up behind the red-bricked walls, iron bars and those tall high walls deliberately covered in shards of broken glass and barbed wire to keep us, children, in and to keep curious, investigative people out.

I was now on the outside in my newly found freedom, hesitant and always on tenterhooks and very wary of those I met on the streets where I now lived full-time with the rest of my family. Due to not seeing my siblings or father that often growing up, I already felt like an outsider and as someone who didn't belong to this family anymore. I was the last one out of the care system, with my sister and two brothers having already been released before me. This meant that they had settled into family life well before me. Now it was time for me to find my place in the fold, as it were, and as the youngest, it was hard to do that when the others were hungrily vying for any small snippet of attention. I now realise, and was sure at that time, that they didn't relish the fact I was now moving into an already crowded house, but once again, I had to learn how to survive this next episode of my life.

My initial feeling was that I was now only an added extra in the family home, feeling my dad had more than enough on his hands, with my three older siblings already at home. I was yet another handful to be added to a recently full house. I felt I was in a house where for many years my dad had probably gotten used to being on his own and in which it was now so obvious that he could no longer cope with too many people around him. He lived in a little two up two down terraced house and had bought this place in preparation for getting us all released from care one day. That day unfortunately didn't come around soon enough for him or us. In fact, it was perhaps much too late for us all. The damage was already done, as my dad, along with ourselves, had suffered immensely back in our early days when we all were taken from him and from our former family home in Newtownbreda on the Saintfield Road.

We siblings had a strange on-off relationship, not truly realising nor wanting to ever talk about what had happened and why we were taken and placed in an institution. It just wasn't spoken of. We never dared to mention our mother or where she went to either. Holding all these natural queries to ourselves, though in reality desperately wanting answers to our inner groanings, we didn't dare to speak of it or to ask my dad questions. Already knowing somehow that between us, we had an unspoken mutual understanding that it was such a taboo subject, to show any interest at all or to declare any intention or emotion of wanting to know anything about her or of her whereabouts.

We could often see the sadness on my dad's face and notice his anxiety and, at times, frustration as he tried his best to provide us with tasty dinners and in carrying out other family domestic matters for us all. We were always allowed a cat; my brother even had bantam hens out back. I recall, at one time, not knowing or being too sure where the hens went as they just suddenly disappeared! Maybe the cat was hungry and had a feast of them as they all lived in the small backyard. Many times, I had my cat in bed with me, and not understanding the ways of the world of males and females and the reproductive systems, either in humans or animals...what had happened overnight astounded me when I awoke to soft meows of tiny little baby kittens stuck into my sides in my bed. I had rolled over unintentionally on one, with its strange hairless body lying there, lifeless. I hid the now-dead kitten in a drawer for ages and wrapped it up in my sister's garment before burying it in the backyard after she had screamed out loudly on seeing it in her drawer. The long-dead body of the kitten looked like a skinny crinkled sausage.

We all attended different schools at first due to our age difference. After dad had woken us up in the early morning before he left for work, he always left our bus fares and lunch monies sitting on the black wrought iron fireplace to be shared amongst us, our names written carefully as to whom owned which set of coins, the older getting the most, I recall. I suppose we began getting somewhat used to each other, even though there was a struggle with whoever wanted to show they were the older, hence being the boss. It wasn't easy living there with a full house, and I must say I was not overly upset when my brothers were put back into a training school on alternative periods. More attention and room and food for me, I thought.

Even though I had got to know a few girls in the area where my dad had his house whilst out on various weekends from the convent, it was still a very distressing time trying to fit in with people in the surrounding streets and those who were completely different to me, or so I believed. How was I going to get along with yet another new world of people, much larger and more numerous than those I had grown up with? How could I manage this without allowing myself to be harmed and ill-treated all over again? Full time living on the outside was very strange, knowing I was out for good and realising I wasn't going back inside was hard to take in or to believe. For many years, I had gotten used to and fully accepted that I always had to go back to the orphanage after previous outings, so this strange, newly found freedom created in me a new kind of fear and dread of the unknown.

As a young eleven-year-old girl, this was very disturbing as I think back on my seemingly being left to my own strategic planning and management of my future life. My learned mistrust of others led me to be watchful and cautious of the actions and behaviour of those around me. I was always hyper-vigilant and on the alert. This migration-like moving around to various dwelling places affected me greatly, with my already younger years having been unsettled, being removed from one settled home to another, that which was anything but settled. And now I would have to learn once again how to cope with the unsettling unknown that lay ahead of me. Just what type of future I was heading into, this time round...I would soon find out!

Not long after I'd been *discharged*, as the religious orders described my being released from their care, I dearly wanted to roam about in the new freedom I was now experiencing, daring to step outdoors and I began trying to find my feet. I didn't bother with many other children, as I overly imagined they were looking at me strangely. From the outset, I felt I was labelled, leading to thinking that everyone else in the school I had just enrolled in knew of my past and somehow knew where I came from, making me feel inferior and inadequate. Mixing with them was traumatising, not having grown up with any of them, as I tried to fit in and find my place amongst them all. Somehow, I knew I would have to settle in, though constantly feeling embarrassed and ashamed, I had always thought that I sort of stuck out, like I had something attached to me, believing I was unclean with an awful disease and that people could see right through me when they stared.

Now, after finding my feet a little, I clowned around a lot, if only to cover the vulnerability I felt deep down. Even at that young age, as an early teen starting secondary school, I hid behind my mask, hoping that no one could see through me, praying that they wouldn't ever know my past, my shame, my secrets.

I pretended not to know any of the girls from the care home whom the nuns had sent for further education to the same secondary school I now attended as a newly freed person. And on seeing any of them who came to the school as first-years, I tried to hide and escape lest they speak to me. Walking along with my head downwards and inwards towards the walls, my now much longer hair which helped cover my face, helped in hoping I wouldn't be recognised. I wanted to hide my past life, thinking to myself if any of the home girls came over to me, then others in the school would obviously know my secrets and hear that I was an ex-home girl too. The shame of others knowing would just be unbearable.

I had a few close friends when I lived in the care home, though on seeing them in my now same school on the outside, I couldn't bear to continue our friendship. I could envisage people asking questions as to how I knew them. So, I pretended I didn't know them and denied knowing any of the girls from Nazareth House throughout my life. I deliberately ignored them all or reacted with shame if they dared to say they knew me. Many times, I resorted to shouting on the school grounds ordering them to stay away from me, and later in life, in the streets when passing me by, even threatening them; much to my embarrassment now in later years.

As life went on and a few years passed by, because of learning the ways of fending for and protecting myself, not too many dared to come near me anymore. I didn't care what people thought of me or what they whispered to each other about me. 'Let them think what they want was my philosophy'. If fighting back kept me from being attacked by bullies, I was happy with the name my newly formed character had now gotten. It didn't matter to me anymore as for many years I was a nobody, and now I felt I was a somebody, albeit on my own, myself alone, in my newly found ways of surviving and a person who wasn't going to allow anyone to hurt me anymore. I was standing up for myself and anyone else who I thought was having a hard time also. I started protecting the vulnerable way back then, not knowing or ever daring to think that I would be doing this a long time ahead into my future. In doing so, I felt that those around me respected me more, took an interest in me and wanted to be my friend. I now wondered how this change of perspective was happening after all these years. Was it because I no longer hid away from others, allowing them to bully me? If so, I liked my newly formed character and decided to keep being the new me, or perhaps was this who I really was? I didn't know. I found it hard to distinguish who I was or who I was supposed to be.

Little did I know back then that my 'new persona' wasn't the answer to my problems and that it would ultimately help to add to the ruination of my life. It was only a cover, a thinly veiled mask, that could be easily broken through and uncovered. The more I got hurt, it enabled memories to break through, allowing them to come crawling stealthily back from my past -then the real me, the vulnerable, lost child, would appear once it was exposed.

At those times, I began to feel the shame of my past. I began to think to myself and ask why I was such an awful person? Why did the holy Christian nuns, children and priests not like me? How was it ever allowed that children could be legally dragged into that horrible old dungeon, so brutally and uncaringly and made to live with all those strange dark figures roaming around in black robes? Why did everybody seem to hate me? Why was I always in trouble? Why was I not like other children who had happy, caring families who loved them?

My instinct to cope after so many nightmarish incidents was to tell myself the truth; I was alone in this world, and the world was against me, so therefore, I was going to have to defend myself against them all. If they all thought I was a horribly bad, mad crazy person, then I was going to be that person! I fought back with the lads who knocked around our corners or wherever I found myself roaming. I always thought of myself as one of the lads and their equal and prided myself in knowing I was now a corner gal and had grown into a tomboy. I hated myself, and anyone I felt would come against me, or those who would try to humiliate me or talk about me behind my back. I was now constantly defending myself, always on high alert, ready to fight back before I was set upon.

I had built up a reputation for myself over my early teenage years as a troublemaker, a fighter, if need be, but this new cover was only a protective persona so that others couldn't harm me in any way. Underneath, I was anything but! I stood around the corner of the street with my new pals, running the railway lines with them, adventurous and also life-threateningly dangerous, as we hopped on the back of large lorries, barely hanging on by our fingernails. Cars beeped their horns at us to get off, the lorry speeding up deliberately to knock us off the back tailgate after we jumped on at traffic stops or just stopping in front of us delivering fruit from the corner fruit store. We ran off, lucky to be alive, over to the railway and climbed onto a long black pipe which lay above the railway lines, built in from one wall to the other on the far side where we knew no one else would feel safe in following us. We would walk the lines towards the fast-flowing river Lagan bridge and daringly walked over this too, laughingly though unwisely, egging each other on to walk the plank...almost falling into the water below—yet another lucky escape. Thinking back, I shouldn't be alive right now to tell this tale. I thought

I was invincible and didn't think of the consequences that doing these crazy things would have upon myself or others. I just seriously didn't give it a thought. I didn't think or understand, or perhaps I just didn't care to.

From my early teenage years and still being at secondary school, I often got into trouble with the school authorities as I was never afraid to square up to anyone. As a result, I was always in all kinds of arguments and fights.

The so-called 'Troubles' in Northern Ireland came at a time for me as an already unruly young teenager, always on the lookout for excitement. I got involved in active, sporadic rioting, throwing bricks and bottles at the police and army. We did not really realise what it was all about then as I just copied what other people were doing. I thought it was fun and exciting. I was already confused, but more so now as I grew into my teenage years. It was my way of managing my anger and rage and my way of release from those emotions. It wasn't that I seriously intended to hurt others at will. This was the time of my life when I became notoriously known as 'Mad Maggie'. I went to school during the day, and after school, I immediately removed my school uniform to dress in denim and steel-tipped shoes or boots, ready for the evening and nightly action on the war-torn streets of Belfast. Now this thin shell of protection was beginning to crack wide open; no longer could I contain the immense anger inside me.

In the early term of attending secondary school and being placed into a middle upper moderate class, I began to quite enjoy schoolwork once I put my mind to it. I enjoyed reading, writing, poetry and many other subjects, not realising though that I had enough intelligence about me at the time. No matter how I tried to play the fool and no matter what I was going through, I was always curious and interested in gaining knowledge and learning more. Though I enjoyed my schoolwork, I was easily led into acting the messer, clowning around and joining in on pranks and plots against pupils and teachers. Trouble and chaos seemed to follow me as I was constantly in the middle of it, always the one to be caught and pointed out as the guilty party whilst many of the others got away.

In my second or third year, I was moved up to a top A class; somehow, whether this was to give me a chance to learn much more and keep me out of trouble instead of running around with the other rowdies in my former class, I'm not sure. It did work for a while. After a few years, my behavioural patterns went up and down, with good and bad behaviour periods. The head nun, who was the principal and ran the school, was soon to get fed up with me, as I was sent to her office too often for minor disturbances. I was more than likely making paper planes and pulling the pigtails of all the posher girls, hiding their schoolbooks and pencils, pinching their sharpeners and silly things that made me laugh so much.

One day, on somehow hearing that I was disturbing the teacher who taught the French class, she came barging through the classroom door. This nun, the school principal, dressed in black, small and thin in stature but with a temper and strength of a bulldog, came towards me with her notorious long leather strap. She, in front of thirty young pupils in the classroom, ran after me up and down the aisles of the wooden desks, with me having to jump over them to get away from her, in doing so dislodging whoever was sitting in them at the same time. She was lashing out wildly, beating me with a very long piece of leather. Her face usually very pale, was red with anger and rage as she shouted at me to come back to her. After I gave up running, she removed me forcibly from the classroom, wielding the strap frantically across my back, my legs and my arms as she herded me out like I was some animal on a farm.

The children in the class were traumatised watching this and were in tears screaming for her to stop hurting me. I was told this years later by some of those children who are now adults who had witnessed it all. Also, I was told that one of the teachers told the pupils never to tell anyone what they had seen. Just recently, I've met girls who were in that class who now have top positions in the media or work as teachers themselves. They reminded me of this incident and the teacher who ordered them to say nothing. Needless to say, that after that episode, I was never brought back to my French class ever again.

The next term, I was placed in a 'special class' for disturbed delinquents by the principal nun, which was how some of the teachers described it, not me. I was first into this class after being brought up on the stage on a Monday morning, the start of the new week and term, in front of the whole school full of pupils and teachers. This was the worst mark you could get for bad behaviour or giving back cheek to any of the teachers. There were also excellent effort marks given out by teachers for good or special behaviour. At times I was also brought up on stage for these. Indeed, many times I received both in one week, causing great conflict all around once again. After a while, this humiliation had no effect on me, as I joked and laughed on the stage and made mocking signs behind the principal nun's back, with all the children below the stage noticeably giggling and laughing out loud. When the principal turned round to look at me to catch me out, I stood straight with an air of innocence, one which she knew was obviously an act, but she didn't catch me. I believe some of the teachers at the back even fought back a giggle as I danced around behind her back like a clown.

The principal and the heads of the school had gotten together in a plan of action as to how to cope with those involved in repetitive bad behaviour and to decide what disruptive pupils should be sent to this new special class! It was to be run and managed solely by another nun who was specifically brought in to stand up to the misfits, the disturbed children or, in essence, just kids who needed direction, understanding and the desire to be treated with a little respect, just as teachers and nuns said they too, should be treated.

She was Sister J. She was the only other nun in the school besides the little bulldog with the long leather strap. Sister J, after settling in and getting to know who was in her special class, took to me strangely enough. We seemed to form a bond and had a mutual understanding of each other. I believe she understood my sense of humour, my tongue-in-cheek attitude and perhaps that was because she was once like me or craved to have been allowed to be so. I also detected a little devilment in her attitude; she wasn't like any of the other nuns I had known. She was more of a human being with a loud, humorous, corner boy manner, strutting around with her sleeves rolled up and baring her fists at us in her feigned threats to keep us quiet. This behaviour from her resonated with me and the rest of the girls. We respected her more so because we were familiar with her attitude and tough gal image.

Sister J placed me in the front seat under her gaze. I suppose that move was deliberate to keep me away from my partners in crime/carnage. She always chose me to read. I loved reading and always had a way with words and adjectives and with spelling and pronunciation. Sister J was pleasant enough with me, but when her eyes narrowed like a wild cat, she was letting me know not to mess her around.

I often saw her scold a few in the class in an unthreatening manner with straps and rulers or anyone who dared to cause any disruption. She was letting us all know, in her class at least, she was the boss and noticed how they immediately stopped swearing at her or misbehaving. I felt they then respected in some small way Sister J, as our newly positioned teacher, who was more like ourselves in a way, with her wicked sense of humour. This eventually allowed her to be thought of as yet another of our ilk, one of us.

Our relationship was an on-off one, each weighing the other up, but each giving one another space and a little freedom to be our own person, whilst perhaps learning to build up some trust in each other; a quite strange relationship but manageable.

When going to lunch breaks or dinners, after earning Sister J's trust, we were allowed as a full class, to walk the corridors unattended or chaperoned, yet knowing the whole school knew we were the bad class, the class no one should go anywhere near, the disrupters and delinquents. I often saw the little first and second years look at us and laugh as they saw us carry on, out of sight of their teachers. Also, the top senior classes seemed to change direction when bumping into our special class, avoiding us lest we tease or torment them.

At one stage, there was a scheme that the principal nun had put in place that if any teachers saw any class walk in the corridors silently and on their best behaviour, they would get a range of coloured stars, gold being the highest. Sister J put her trust in us at this stage, taking a risk, now knowing I was the somehow promoted prefect of our class. I chose someone weekly as our sub-prefect, who, when either of us saw a teacher coming along, helped push everyone back into line again, immediately keeping quiet, walking perfectly straight, with heads in the air, knowing we would get a star. Doing so, we would be almost bursting with laughter as we turned the corner and got out of the teacher's vision, and then we rolled over in near hysterics. We had them all conned. This class was so much fun and the best one I was ever in, and all our lovable misfits agreed. A class of our own, the top class of clowns who had so much respect and trust in each other, we reminded ourselves in the years ahead, that we were like the Schoolgirls of St Trinian's.

After school, I returned to spend the rest of my evenings hanging around the corners. I always carried a transistor radio with me, and I loved music, knowing every word of every song that was in the charts. Radio Luxemburg fed all the hits at night, as did Radio 1 during the daytime. The 'Troubles' still ravaged on, I did not truly understanding why police and army were on the streets outside our houses, or why they blocked the roads with their Saracens and army jeeps! The soldiers shouted obscenities at us all, even young school children, rounding up men and women, arresting them after we watched them ransack houses and raid pubs and clubs in the area.

This was my escape route once again, my chance to get rid of some of my real anger and the rage that had been welling up in me for all these years! Whenever there was a riot, I was at the front of the crowd. I'd learnt how to precisely throw bricks, or 'halfers' as we called them, at our targets. The pavements had all been raised and broken up in pieces for the readymade armoury our gangs would use to attack the enemy. As a tomboy, I enjoyed collecting bonfire wood, just as we had watched our older siblings and others in the neighbourhood do before our coming of age. Now, we were the ones climbing into collapsed buildings, empty houses, or anywhere that we could strip it of its wood, furniture or anything that could be salvaged. These were used for barricades or to burn on our piled high pre-prepared stashes that we stored against the walls adjacent to an old railway line, which of course was my former childhood haunt.

We made makeshift houses, or dens as we called them, all childhood fun with a devil-may-care attitude. We had our own make-believe territory that we had our own authority over, as it were. Growing up, I oversaw many of the fires; all the crowd in the area had known I never left the stash and protected it furiously from anyone who would dare to hijack what we worked hard for. If they only knew why? This was my release from the frustration that I'd built up inside of me. Nothing or no one would stop me from doing what I wanted to do. I feared no one, and deep inside, I was angry, and that's what fuelled the adrenaline that kept me going. I had an inner strength in this anger as I didn't have to answer to anyone now. The rioting I took part in was my life now. I didn't know any better. I got drunk on bottles of cider, and every police officer and regiment of soldiers knew me so well that they regularly introduced me to the next new regiment on tour. As they passed me on the roads in their jeeps and Saracens, they would shout my name out loud for all to hear, and I would throw anything at them in response. I even acquired eggs somehow and pelted them over the heads of people from atop of the railway wall. They often tried to catch me but couldn't, as I knew the railway tunnel and its shortcuts into the side streets and alleyways in our surrounding area. They hadn't a clue how to find or catch me as I ran faster than an antelope.

I recall one of the many incidents after one particular huge bonfire night, which, of course, brought rioting on the road. The army swooped early morning upon myself and other stragglers hanging around the corners, standing by our still half-lit fire. Several of us were gathered there, warming ourselves at the still glowing embers and ashes from the many tyres, doors, window frames and mattresses that we had thrown on from the night before. Suddenly, there was a sound of the army jeeps and Saracens coming, driving noisily at full speed as they careered recklessly towards us, almost running us down. They knew who they wanted to arrest, and as I and others ran up and down the streets, and after avoiding capture for an hour or so, they pounced and caught me and then handed me over to the police. This was in the early days of my unruly lifestyle. What was about to occur made me distraught as the undercover, unmarked police car began the drive to the so-called Good Shepherd Convent facing Nazareth House. My stomach churned, and the shame of it came rapidly back to me, making me reel in embarrassment after I was told I was to be remanded by the courts into their custody. This triggered what I now know as Post Traumatic Stress Disorder (PTSD).

I couldn't believe it; out of all the places to be remanded in custody, it was always to those people, albeit a different order of nuns...the religious orders...who had already caused me so much trauma, emotional pain and suffering. Going through those gates made me so ill, mentally; triggers from the past and of being resident in Nazareth House directly across the street instantly came back to me. Seeing the red-bricked walls surrounding it brought back many memories, even though I was now entering the so-called Good Shepherd Convent, which was hedged in with grey concrete bricks and tall oak and sycamore trees. Many of these women had once been incarcerated across the street in Nazareth House, where I had been, and when allowed to go out alone in society at aged sixteen, the nuns and priests had gotten them jobs as housekeepers, nannies, cleaners or whatever, to the well-heeled congregations of the local churches in the area, one being the Holy Rosary next door to Nazareth House.

This same chapel in which the notorious Canon Murphy shouted and bellowed from the walls of his gardens whenever he caught any of us hungry children daring to climb up to the overhanging branches which bore delicious fruit. The Canon foamed at the mouth as he ran around into the convent to let the nuns know we had dared to steal his precious fruit and demanded we be kept away from his trees. This indeed brought us into great trouble as, once again the nuns were humiliated at the sight of the most Holy Reverend Canon Murphy being disturbed from his rest time after eating his 'fit for a king' five-course meal that the clergy were accustomed to. This in contrast to what those on the other side of the wall of his mansion had to eat, or not...the forgotten, hungry children, begging to eat the scraps of the table. No doubt, in the minds of the Church and the Religious Orders, this was what we rightly deserved, a righteous divine penance for the unholy sins of our parents, such was their pompous, condescending manner!

Meanwhile, the police car sat outside the eerie Good Shepherd Convent building after the seemingly never-ending journey up the long road that I knew so well, a road I had walked down not that long ago when I was released from Nazareth House. I had just come from the Townhall Street Court Police detention cells that smelled of urine, stale vomit and the putrid stench of body odour. I was driven through an area I knew so well; this was my neighbourhood they chose to drive me through en-route to where the police were about to transfer me. I kept my head down low, horrified that if anyone caught sight of me...Maggie in a cop car. What would people think in a time when no one could ever dare to be seen near police or the army?

As the large front door was opened and I was brought into the reception area, a nun came through yet another large dark brown creaky door, which noisily scraped along the cemented stone floor beneath it. The cops handed me over after I'd tried to wrench myself out of their grip, calling them the best and worst of my foulest choice language I'd learnt on the streets, of which I, Maggie, was very proud! Seeing these nuns, even of a different religious order, made me feel angry and upset. They were still the same to me. Strange-looking creatures, eerily dressed in black habits from head to toe, with their eyes just about showing through underneath their veils.

So, here I was once again, back in an institution as an almost 15 year old young teenager, retraumatised because the authorities thought it was appropriate to lock me away on again and remand me under their 'care', until my next court appearance. I was brought to a cell-like room not much different to the cell I'd just stayed in overnight. A girl who was obviously resident in the convent was ordered to bring me upstairs to my room, telling me teatime was over, so I wouldn't get anything to eat until morning. I felt like immediately thumping her, daring to talk to me in that bossy boot's manner. She sounded exactly like someone from where I had once been resident, and I knew this place was so like Nazareth House that I planned to get out of it as soon as possible.

I tried to get a good look around the building when I went to the bathrooms that night and again the next morning at breakfast. I was determined to get out of it somehow! I kept staring out the windows, in tears, but wouldn't dare allow anyone to see the tears falling down my face to the wooden floors at my feet. Looking out the windows, I could clearly see Nazareth House Convent facing me. The red brick and the tall green trees triggered me in some way, bringing back so many awful memories of my time spent in that horrible building from the age of just over three until I was eleven. Eight very long years spent behind those walls, day in and out, 24/7 staring at the same walls, a few trees, the same nuns dressed in black, the same inedible food, the same punishments and beatings, humiliation and torture!

As I now stood in the cold hallway by the window, not one person came to ask me how I was or why I was standing looking out the windows and not mixing with the others. Such was the coldness of attitude built into the residents along with the building. I certainly wasn't going to mix and settle with anyone; I wanted out! After a few days on remand there, I'd got talking to one girl who seemed to know what exactly was on my mind...escape! She divulged that she got caught leaving the premises and was brought back by the cops. I asked her how to get out, and she motioned to a back door downstairs to the back of the building. I craned my neck around the back of the building, wondering where it would lead me to. I soon got the courage to walk or tiptoe down the stairs hoping no one would see me doing so. I had to pretend I was lacing my shoes whenever someone would pass on the stairs, ignoring their curious glances and queries to each other as to what I was doing and where I was going. At last, I found the back door and flew out of it, sidling up to the long adjacent walls where shrubs and bushes had lined the whole way to a door that I was determined to reach, hiding down low beneath the bushes and undergrowth, I darted in and out of them, till until I got to the door. It was open. I found out later that it was used for staff, delivery men and nuns who oversaw the Mother and Baby Unit.

I was out and ran around the back residential area, not daring to go out to the Ormeau Road, where the nuns were more likely to see me. After an hour or more, I somehow found my way down the long road to my very good friend's house. The lady of the house was surprised to see me, as was the family. They had all been told about my arrest but didn't know where I was as the police wouldn't tell them. When I told them I'd broken out of the Good Shepherd Convent, they were very supportive of me but, in wisdom, told me that if I didn't go back, I'd receive a far longer sentence for breaking out than I would for my riotous or disorderly behaviour charges alone. They promised to find me a place to stay and that if I got a prison sentence, I could appeal it and then go on the run, as it were. I agreed to sneak back into the convent after they drove me close to the building at the back door; luckily, it was still open. I thought no one noticed my disappearance. Not a word was spoken to me on my return.

I made my next appearance in court, and my defence solicitor, in answer to the judge's question about why I took leave from the premises, responded that "she was only away a few hours and wanted to look around the buildings". The nuns had written in a statement that I had disappeared for quite a few hours one evening and that most of my time there, I mixed with no one, didn't eat, wouldn't speak to anyone and only stared out windows. This statement was read out in the courtroom. Thank God my charges had been reduced, this time to disorderly behaviour, and I received probation on the premise that I wouldn't get into trouble again. I was free once again, freedom from those in authority, whether it be the church, the religious orders, or the police.

This did not stop my disturbing behavioural traits. Even though I tried very hard, I didn't know what else to do. I felt I was uncontrollable and didn't understand the reasons why I was the way I was. I continued my activities after school; again, I was remanded in custody into a juvenile detention centre, this time in Middletown on the Co. Armagh border, another institution run by another religious order, heavens above!

Around this time, after I received probation and suspended sentences, I gave up wanting to go to school. I did have some fun at school and did crazy things, like finding a way of setting of the alarm bells in the corridors, which had a specific warning sound that I had learnt. On hearing this specific sound, the teachers knew to clear the classrooms. If it didn't work, I used to bang on all the classroom doors saying it was a bomb scare or a fire, this only to get the pupils out of class whilst I was filled with laughter. I remember when it was snowing heavily outside, I made giant snowballs and managed to carry or roll them indoors and leave them outside certain teachers' classrooms, always in fits of laughter. I was a clown with a painted-on face, but underneath, I still didn't know who or what I was or where I was going then or in the future! I had linked in with others who knew where to hide away instead of going to school. They used to pinch out of small shops, stealing food and sweets. I hadn't done that before, though I soon got in the way of it the more I ran about with these girls. Always nervous but felt I had to do so to keep in with this new group of friends. I felt my life was changing. I was growing up and venturing further afield, as it were. I didn't go back to school as my last few months there were almost over. I'm sure the teachers were happy enough to be rid of me, especially the principal nun and the vice principal, who were as wicked as each other with their painful corporal punishment every morning. My life was now on a new path with new people, though I didn't know where I would end up in this chapter of my life. I would soon find out, and it wasn't where I expected it to be. Life for Maggie wasn't plain sailing or wasn't going to get any easier. Indeed, more of the same and much worse lay in the months and years ahead!

CHAPTER FOUR

A s the years went by, I began to take refuge in older friends' company. Those I had befriended were quite a few years older than me. I could no longer stand being around children my age, strongly feeling the need to find my feet elsewhere. Wanting to grow up fast and be considered an older teenager, I suddenly broke away from my old school friends. I now also wanted to call an end to my tomboy mannerisms, activities, dress code and childish pranks. I had no desire at all to remain where I was at present in my life. I'd left school. I felt I had outgrown my corner girl wild child escapades. I was done with street brawls, stone-throwing and fighting with the army and police. I now had enough of my addictive behaviours of protecting our street corners and collecting bonfire wood.

My friends and I had previously gotten into the habit where we would all congregate in the local alleyways on weekends, boys in one alley and the girls in another close by, always a time to dress up and catch up while drinking a few bottles of cider. A time of singing our hearts out after the buzz of the cider took hold, howling like alley cats as we sat on the old cold steps of the neighbouring backyards. Any song that was handed down from our older sisters or friends, we crowed it aloud, quite often to the after-chorus refrains of local people shouting at us to take ourselves off. Our response to them was to kick their back doors as we ran away shouting obscenities at the neighbours who had come out to chase us down the darkened alley, hoping they would catch us. Of course, they never could. After our cider bottles had been drunk and emptied between us, we went off to find and join up with the boys in their alleyway, often scrounging cider off them as they always had more than us. Many of the lads had jobs and the money to buy plenty more. The usual routine was to head onwards to the local Italian chippy, meeting up with other stragglers along the way, always to the sounds of sirens from police and army jeeps. It was then the usual street fighting would break out as bricks and bottles were thrown at the military, the young men and whoever stood around the corners, taking a grudge to the armoured tanks and police jeeps sitting around parked up on footpaths. Military personnel would jump out and search them after forcibly making them lay spreadeagled on the cold ground, often striking them with rifle butts. With arrests made overnight and into the early mornings, this was what it was like growing up in many areas at this time, weekends being the worst.

It was around then, after the fun had begun to wear off, that I so much wanted to get away from the area I was living in. The dynamics and population were dramatically changing. Many old friends were growing up and moving out, with families leaving the district and new people moving in. I wanted to race ahead quickly in the search for whatever the world and the future held for me, if I could ever find it. In doing so, I got into pubs and clubs early, sitting with my older friends feeling more grown up.

Getting to know the day-to-day activities of my older friends was eye-opening because of their antics. They would steal out of various shops, and I would watch them closely to see that they didn't have to pay for anything, laughing as they ran out with their ill-gotten gains spilling out of their pockets and from under their armpits.

After a while, they coaxed and encouraged me to do the same if I wanted to have what they had. Even though I was always very nervous, I began mimicking what they did, knowing I'd be left behind and friendless if I didn't. Not wanting to return to my younger group of friends, I agreed to join in by pinching small items, mainly makeup, which I put under my arms. Navigating successfully to find the front door and escape unchallenged gave me a buzz.

To get away with it in front of unsuspecting shop assistants was a victory of sorts and made me feel confident at times, more so when my newly found friends praised me for doing so, making me feel accepted and one of them. The more I did it and got away with it, the more praise I received, and it made me feel invincible, although I still felt out of my depth. I never felt good about doing it, I did feel guilty, and it often showed on my face. I blushed, almost giving myself away as I hurried out the exit doors of whatever shops we went into. These little shopping sprees would gradually become more adventurous as we went along. Firstly, we would steal out of any small shop, anywhere at any time and in doing so, I imagined I was now an adult and much wiser in the world. Such was my immaturity in my unwise thinking at that time.

In moving forward and naively thinking I had become more experienced in my newest trait, we would go into Belfast town centre to meet up in our selected bars, whereby many other well-known "schemers" would be hanging around. This was the nickname back in the mid-1970s, and early 1980s that minor crime gangs were given.

At this stage, we would go into larger stores and shopping centres acquiring clothes and whatever else was on hand or view, this of course, to naïve teenagers was always inviting and an invitation or offer to feel free to avail of the items for ourselves. Many of the gangs sold their haul of goods to strangers in the side streets or back rooms and toilets of pubs on the edges of town. For others, after being informed that a particular shop was a "gift", meaning not many staff were on or with no door staff or security, dutifully went to the stores marked out for them by their associates. This is where we got to know each other, from areas all over Belfast and further afield. Many had just gotten out of prison and needed money for food, alcohol, cigarettes and clothes; this was the only profession many knew of.

Problems arose not too long after I started going into the city centre. I was terribly gullible and not realising or entirely aware that certain store detectives or floor walkers would follow any suspecting shoplifters, stop and arrest them if need be. Being relatively new at this and not knowing those who policed the stores or what they looked like was a big concern. Also, not knowing that they wore plain clothes, like daily shoppers, was much harder to deal with.

The first time a friend and I got caught by a male and female detective, we didn't realise who they were even though, at this particular time, we somehow knew we were being followed. We disappeared in and out of pubs to get away from them, and thinking we got rid of them, we walked back around the streets to get out of town. That's when they caught up with us. The detectives then asked to look into our bags after saying they believed we left a store without paying for clothing items. On seeing nothing was parcelled up correctly or with a receipt, they asked us to accompany them to the police station.

These detectives always roamed about in stores to prevent bomb devices from being planted inside clothing and to be on the lookout for anyone acting suspiciously in or outside the stores in all town centres in Northern Ireland because of the ongoing 'Troubles' at the time. My new friend and I were arrested by these undercover cops and charged with theft, and that was the beginning of my new stage in life, on the wrong road that I had very unwisely chosen. I now ended up in the adult petty sessions court, which was a big shock, as I didn't want to keep getting into trouble and arrested again and again. This time, however, as it was the first-time offence of shoplifting, I received a fine.

After this unsavoury episode, I did try to break away from my unsuitable friends and associates, attempting to settle down and get 'honest' work. I was employed in various stitching factories, which I detested because of the boredom and being told what to do. Of course, I didn't last long in these jobs and was off again, searching for another in between times. Then I came upon a job I genuinely liked: flower arranging and wreath making, located in the local area near where I was from. I enjoyed this new walk of life very much and made new friends who worked alongside me.

The job was based in a building situated in an area of mixed communities over three-floor levels. Yet somehow, I could keep my head down, get to work, and we all managed to get along. I had been there for about four months when a couple of my former associates phoned up and asked my boss if they could pass an urgent message to me, stating that my father had been in a serious accident and they had called to get me to come to the hospital straight away. This had been made up to get me out to go into the town with them. As usual, I didn't know what was happening at the time.

The boss gave me his deepest sympathies and said to me very emotionally, almost tearful and upset...that if he could help me in any way, he would and sent his best wishes to my father, praying he would get well soon. I found it very strange why anyone would contact me, as I was the youngest in a family of four.

As I left the workplace and closed the front door, the two who had made the call stood around a corner, laughing at the idea that they had phoned up in pretence just to get me out of work. I got out of work all right but found myself allowing them to lure me back to the town centre. 'Just for a walk,' they said. Still, I knew it would be shoplifting again with these two and of course, it was too late to return to work, as I couldn't tell my boss the truth...and certainly not after his public display of sympathy towards me over my supposedly injured father's falsified accident.

After being pressured to go with them and feeling too weak to refuse, I agreed to walk into town with them, not wanting to be a spoilsport or be considered a coward. This led to the restart of pinching out of the shops, and because of my weakness beneath my hardened façade, I just could not possibly say no! As we walked through the town centre, with the regular army and civilian search teams present at the stop and search checkpoints, we, unwisely and immaturely, but bold as brass, wandered on, thinking no one would notice us with our bags filled with stolen goods. Soldiers were only looking for bombing materials and devices and to protect the town from bombers and paramilitaries, we thought.

This was a regular part of the daily public search because of the conflict. Therefore, because of this and knowing we were not bombers, we blatantly and brazenly walked through the security gates, assuming none of them would be interested in the innocent contents of our carrier bags. It was one of the British Army red caps that I, on seeing her whispering to a colleague, walked towards me, stopped me and pulled me over to one side.

The military policewoman questioned me about where I got the clothing in my carrier bags and why the items weren't wrapped up. I aggressively shouted at her that I was at the open street markets stalls and had bought them. I thought to myself..."That's me arrested". On looking for my other two associates who had initially persuaded me into going back to my old ways and haunts, I noticed they had long gone. They had gotten through the barriers unchallenged, whereas I stood captured, cornered. I had been caught, once again; oh, how foolish could I have been to allow myself to be coaxed into going out in the first place? Suddenly, her male MP colleague openly agreed that you do not always get shopping wrapped up in the street markets, saying market stalls don't give receipts either. I was amazed and fortunate to get off that time. He certainly had something against his female colleague, who must have known me from my earlier escapades. But unfortunately, this unwanted episode cost me my job, my chance in a million of settling down to do something I, for once in my life, truly enjoyed.

No matter how much I liked being in the flower-arranging business, I didn't return to my job. I was too embarrassed to walk back to work, knowing it was a lie that had been told. I suppose being used by others and the lies they told to get me out of work had upset me. I felt for my now former boss, as he was so kind and caring towards me. How could I tell him it was a lie? I just couldn't face him as I was so embarrassed and ashamed. My fellow workers had recently said to me that the manager was very proud of my work record. I had taken to making wreaths and flower arranging very quickly and he noticed how I had perfectly made up the displays. For once, I could have been settled in a job, but the choice was taken from my hands purely because I had made wrong decisions again, hanging around with the wrong people, thinking I knew better. I thought, "Being settled isn't ever going to be the plan or part of my life's future, it seems!"

Not long after that, yet another close shave and an almost further arrest by the police, I began praying outwardly for the strength, wisdom and courage to stay away from trouble so that I could somehow find peace and genuine, safe friendships in my life. Wishing I could have been sensible enough to refuse to go out with these former friends, I decided to stay away from these in particular. But once again, because of either boredom or selective amnesia, I found myself unwittingly and unwisely somehow being drawn into the company of others I knew of in the broader circle of friends or associates who roamed around a particular area close to the town centre.

We were hanging around with each other when there was nothing else to do in life. We all needed money, food and clothes, and that's where and how we formed our unsuitable convenient friendships. Few opportunities were available, and I didn't have the guidance to be directed to them. It appeared that everyone I knew was involved in crime of some sort, which seemed to be just a way of life in those days. The 'Troubles' were raging, unemployment was rife, money was scarce, and the world seemed chaotic.

I had lived in my dad's house only at certain times, usually when I wasn't running around the town centre and staying periodically in friends' houses. I didn't want to be at the family home. I felt estranged from my siblings and dad and wanted to be anywhere but there. I didn't know then that it was because of memories of being in care, which I didn't want to be reminded of. My friend's sister-in-law moved into the next street over from mine, and we were introduced. She was a professional shoplifter who hated capitalists. She stated, "It is ok to rob the rich of their millions and to provide for the poor and unkempt". I agreed. We became great friends, and I moved into her squatter's house rent-free, with everything supplied free of charge. She and I went to bars after our daily sprees in various town centres, and a few others always tagged along too. My new friend was indeed a professional. She was straight in and out of shops with bags full of anything the awaiting penniless customers required. She often gave clothing to people experiencing poverty. This went on for quite a while, with me getting to know the ropes and meeting many others in the same profession.

It was like back in the times of Dickens...waifs and strays around the town centre begging or thieving for clothing or something to eat. Such were the times. I continued shoplifting and was caught again, as I was never up to the standard at that stage to be as alert as she was. I didn't get probation, a fine, or conditional discharge this time. I received a prison term and was sentenced to three months in Armagh jail. This was probably because of my record of other criminal behaviours and because I was very late for the court hearing as I was perched in the back of a bar at the corner of Chichester Street, knocking back Vat 19 rum with two friends who accompanied me.

The judge wasn't pleased with me and sentenced me in my absence, while my solicitor 'pleaded guilty', accepting the three months prison sentence on my behalf. I wasn't savvy about the courts' system, but if I'd known, I would have appealed this sentence myself, but the solicitor told me the judge wouldn't allow the appeal, telling me, "Aw sure, the three months will fly by, and by the time the appeal is up you will be back out again". I was immediately brought downstairs and put into the urine-soaked, vomit-filled court cells in Townhall Street at the back of the courthouse. This time it was to be doing time, big time. I was undoubtedly old enough, as I wanted to be...though now at this moment I wished I was only a very young child again and back with my parents and siblings in my first and former happy family home, although this was never to be again.

I didn't know what the inside of an actual prison looked like. My earlier visions of the prison were of those dungeon-like places we had been sent to at Nazareth and the buildings we stayed in on our rare holiday occasions with the nuns. This place I was now being driven to by uniformed wardens in an unmarked prison van was in the City of Armagh, fifty or more miles from Belfast. It was an ancient castle-like fortress with very high grey stone walls with barbed wire covering the outsides and inside walls in separate wings of the building. As I was led into the old grey stone floor cell with walls painted in the identical sickly colours of the religious orders' dwellings, I thought I was going back in time. Once again, I was put back into familiar surroundings.

On being placed into a cell, I immediately caught sight of two single wrought iron beds lining each wall with a tiny narrow window high up near the ceiling, metal bars covering up the tiny window. No chance of escaping from here, I thought to myself. I was told I would share it with another person, and she looked to me like a very old woman, which shocked me. I wondered why or how an older woman could be in prison and whatever for. I had only recently turned the age of which I was now old enough to go to jail and not a youth detention centre anymore.

I stayed in my cell for a few days trying to take in where I was, hoping and praying again; it was a bad dream, and I would awaken from my fitful sleep. Now and then, I dared to come out and stand at the heavy steel door, arms folded and acting like I was unafraid and not upset at being in this large, strange prison with uniformed wardens wandering up and down and the sound of heavy metal keys and steel doors being banged closed as they did their duty to the crown. I was trying to suss people out and see if I knew any people who wandered around the landings or up and down the caged staircases leading to the upstairs landings. I soon got to know a crowd of girls and older women from an opposite area in South Belfast, quite near the area that I was from. These women of all ages were in for kidnapping and murdering a woman. They lived near the old road I was originally from before my wanderings. One of the girls in the next cell to mine came over and spoke to me, giving me cigarettes. That's when I came out of my shell and out of my cell. I was sentenced to three months, but she told me I would only spend two months inside with time off for good behaviour, something I was delighted to hear.

For exercise, we could walk around the square outside when given permission. We were allowed to walk around for an hour or so. It was lovely to get out to walk in the fresh air or watch TV in the association room. I was unaware that two individuals had their own marked-out chairs for themselves, with no one else daring to sit in these two chairs closest to the TV. I walked into the room and inadvertently sat on one of the chairs in front of the TV, and one of the girls, who thought they were hard women, came charging in. She was shouting that I was sitting in her seat, which made me angrier than she was, as I called back to her, "Oh right, is your name on it?" and I refused to get up. This surprised her as everyone else knew on the lower landing that this was her seat and didn't dare sit there, afraid of being bullied by her and her loudmouth threats. I continued sitting on the chair, saying it didn't belong to her. It was a free association room for all. I certainly wasn't going to back down now, fearful as I may have been. I had learned never to allow anyone to bully or threaten me anymore, or else I would be giving them the power to do so in the future. I think I may have been the first to answer her back or challenge her and refuse to move out of the chair, which was not hers. She joked around then in a bemused and flabbergasted manner after I then told her, "I'll let you have it when I'm finished watching the TV programme." She couldn't believe someone had stood up to her and made her feel she was no longer the top dog.

Here I was building friendships with the strangest company to keep friendly with. After that day, we seemed to get along, and I also befriended her fellow loyalist colleagues. We were total opposites from across the religious divide in Belfast and beyond. I was from the Nationalist Catholic area, and these girls were all from the Protestant Unionist Loyalist area. Still, in jail, of all places, we became friends, if only for the remainder of my time alongside them. I didn't realise at that time they were high up in a paramilitary group notorious for many horrific murders of innocent victims. This group of women were involved in a 'Romper Room murder' of a young woman. For this reason, she was 'rompered', a crude term for being set upon and beaten.

On finding out the truth later, as I settled into prison, I did what I had gotten used to doing in my past. I started closing down my thoughts and memory when things got too much for me. I hummed to myself to block out what I had recently heard about these people, trying to get this horrific picture of a young lady set upon and murdered in the worst way one could ever dare to ever imagine out of my mind.

I began chastising myself, saying it's best to knuckle down, do my time, and I'll get out of here with good behaviour sooner and not any later, hopefully, if I can only behave. The female wardens, or 'screws' as we called them, gave us work to do and would've had us doing slave labour every day, with particular ones thriving with their authority over us. I tried my best to abide by the excellent behaviour rules, but many times, I had run-ins with the wardens, which meant I would lose out on association time, bonuses or wages for working. I tried my best to adjust to being in prison or get used to doing work, but because of my past, I hated and detested authority and rebelled against it. I shouted back at the wardens, telling them where to go and going into a mad rage, though this depended on the attitude and manner or how they spoke to me. If it was in a bossy demeaning way, I was triggered immediately and went on the defensive. This behaviour then led me to be put on report, and I had to apologise to all concerned, which was very hard for me to do, but I didn't want to lose out on my early release date.

I suppose what helped ease the pressure and loneliness of serving time was receiving a letter or a visit and catching up on the latest news from the outside. These were my best days inside, as getting a letter made the sentence more manageable. I had written out in letters asking that whoever was visiting me would bring or send in my own clothes. Always the one for dressing up, I had all my suits brought in with blouses and accessories to match.

When newly sentenced prisoners often entered the jail, I would look out for those I may have known from the outside. So, I was there to greet others coming inside and help them adjust just as I had to, as it's not easy for anyone to settle into prison. As I had gotten many of my clothes sent to me, I loaned them to other remanded prisoners when they appeared in court to look well and presentable in the new suits. There were many women there that hadn't any smart clothes to wear for court, so I believed I was providing a service allowing them to dress up on their day out, albeit even on a journey in a prison van, which drove to Belfast city courthouse, placed them into cells before being presented to the court judges. I recall loaning one of the suits quite a few times to the woman up for the murder. Although it was too small, she squeezed into it, keeping the zip and buttons open and hidden with a large blouse. She and many others wanted to look good for their friends, family and partners who would journey to the courtrooms to support each other.

I remember even the prison wardens started asking where I'd gotten so many nice clothes, suits of all colours, with matching accessories and telling them openly and honestly how I had acquired them, then showing them how it was done. Laughing as I taught them how to roll suits or dresses, pairs of jeans or whatever came to hand on our escapades and how to place them into a large bag, we always carried around with us. Looking back, I realise how immature and senseless that was. It showed how lost I was. I had no one to look up to or mentors to advise me. I was always clowning around, pretending

I didn't care about the consequences. Those certain 'screws' thought what I had shown them was hilarious, and we all laughed together and got on quite well even though they knew what I was in prison for. I suppose we all had to spend our time within the same shared building, whatever our background and my time inside taught me how to make life a bit easier for myself by having to knuckle down and have some laughs along the way, at least until I was released. The release date was something I looked forward to more than anything. I counted down every day and every hour by ticking off the boxes on my pretend calendar I had made from a scrap of paper with squares and dates. I stuck it to my prison wall beside my bed, staring at it nightly and praying that my release day would arrive swiftly.

I had various visits from a few friends. I was still quite guarded about whom I would allow into my private life. I had many associates, but not many I could call friends, purposely. Whoever did visit, I was and am eternally grateful to, as this helped prison time go by quicker, especially when looking forward to catching up on the latest news and happenings from the outside of the new walls surrounding me. Being locked away from people was an intentional punishment. To take a person away from the normality of meeting people, taking away one's freedom, family, and friends is extremely difficult to endure. This separation was to act as a deterrent hoping one would learn from it, in not repeating one's activities of criminal behaviour in the future. Unfortunately, on many occasions, I lived the lifestyle of criminality just trying to survive. Hence, the deterrent couldn't stop me from repeating my earlier offences. Why? Because I didn't have a normal or suitable family lifestyle from which to draw resilience.

Margaret McGuckin outside Nazareth House, March 2023
(Photographed by Kevin Cooper).

Margaret McGuckin at Stormont lobbying for HIA Inquiry

(Author's own photograph).

Margaret McGuckin, victorious after winning the high court judicial review for the implementation of the Hart Inquiry findings

(Photograph by Hugh Russell, The Irish News).

Margaret McGuckin from SAVIA at the protest by clerical abuse campaigners outside Belfast City Hall

(Picture Source: Colm Lenaghan/Pacemaker).

Margaret McGuckin bottom left beside Michelle O'Neill and other ministers at the HIA Apology 11 March 2022 in Stormont

(Picture Cool FM via NI Assembly TV Feed).

Margaret McGuckin receiving the Aisling Person of the Year Award 2017
(Photograph by Belfast Media.@newbelfast.com).

Margaret McGuckin and Kate Walmsley at the end of the 15-year battle for justice for survivors and victims of Historical Institutional Abuse

(Photo taken by Hugh Russell, Irish News).

10 DOWNING STREET
LONDON SW1A 2AA
www.gov.uk/Number10

From the Direct Communications Unit

16 November 2017

Ms Margaret McGuckin

████████

Belfast

████████

Dear Ms McGuckin

I am writing on behalf of the Prime Minister to thank you and your co-signatories for your letter of 3 November.

Mrs May very much appreciates the time you have taken to write to her.

As the Northern Ireland Office has responsibility for the matters you raise, I am forwarding your letter to them so that they are aware of your views.

Thank you, once again, for writing.

Yours sincerely

Francesca

Correspondence Officer

**Northern
Ireland
Office**

Secretary of State for
Northern Ireland
1 Horse Guards Road
London
SW1 2HQ
T 020 7210 6455
T 02890 160206

Stormont House
Belfast
BT4 3SH

E SoS.Smith@nio.gov.uk
www.gov.uk/nio
Follow us on Twitter @NIOgov

Margaret McGuckin
Via email: survivorsni@gmail.com

8 November 2019

Dear Margaret,

I am delighted to report that the Bill successfully passed through its final stages in the House of Commons and received Royal Assent on 5 November.

Passing this Bill is a hugely positive step towards securing that redress that victims and survivors deserve and have waited upon for so long.

I am conscious of the fact that this is not the end of the journey and more time and effort is needed to quickly establish the Redress Board to make the payments to victims that are so long overdue.

To this end a project management team has been created by the Northern Ireland Civil Service. This team will take forward the work on the implementation of the Commissioner and the Redress Board. David Sterling, the Head of the NI Civil Service, and the Executive Office have already met to see how things can be expedited and I will be continuing to engage with David Sterling to discuss the progress made on implementation.

I know that the tireless campaigning of victims groups has been instrumental in delivering this legislation. Your dedication and commitment in seeking justice for those without a voice is an inspiration to us all. I therefore want to take this opportunity to wholeheartedly thank you for taking the time to meet with myself, my predecessors and my officials as we have worked towards this day.

**RT HON JULIAN SMITH MP
SECRETARY OF STATE FOR NORTHERN IRELAND**

MARGARET MCGUCKIN

RT HON JULIAN SMITH MP
Skipton & Ripon

HOUSE OF COMMONS
LONDON SW1A 0AA

Ms Margaret McGuckin
▓▓▓▓▓▓▓▓▓ Grove
Belfast
BT12 ▓▓▓▓

25 February 2020

Dear Margaret,

Thank you so much for your very kind email, but also for the incredible and humbling support you have given me in the media.

The fact that you took the time to write articles and go onto the radio and television in support of my work as Northern Ireland Secretary means so much to me.

I look forward to staying in touch and please don't hesitate to let me know if there is anything I can help you with in the future.

With thanks again and kind regards,

Rt Hon Julian Smith CBE MP

Tel: 020 7219 7145 · Email: julian.smith.mp@parliament.uk · Website: www.juliansmith.org.uk

The Right Honourable Jacob Rees Mogg MP
Leader of the House of Commons
The Palace of Westminster
London SW1A 0AA

Dear Mr Mogg,

As a Catholic priest I represented the Diocese of Down and Connor at the Historical Institutional Abuse Inquiry in Northern Ireland. Down and Connor owned two of the Children's Homes at the centre of the Inquiry's investigations. It is a matter of deep personal shame for me and for the Diocese that both homes were found by the Inquiry to have fundamentally failed the children in their care, enabling regimes of horrific and systemic emotional, physical and sexual abuse of children, as well as neglect.

In the period before the Inquiry, I came to know some of the former residents of these homes and publicly supported them in their calls for justice and an Inquiry. Over the years of the Inquiry and since, I have watched as those who led this campaign and the hundreds of former children in care who took part in the Inquiry relived the horrors of their time in these institutions and the abuse they suffered there. As children, they arrived at these homes frightened, disorientated and with the simple hope of every child that the adults in their lives with respond to them with affection, understanding, tenderness and care. Instead, they were met so often with hard-hearted coldness, harsh regimes of sterile adult routine and love lessness, as well as indescribable sexual and physical abuse. It is difficult to over state the suffering that the former residents of these homes have endured and continue to endure as a result of their experience.

It has been tragic and heart-breaking beyond words to watch those same children, now as adults, having to face repeated and inexcusable set back after set back as elected representatives in Northern Ireland, and now in Westminster, fail to give the needs of these courageous survivors of child abuse and their search for justice the absolute priority it deserves.

It is for this reason that I write to appeal to you in the strongest possible terms, appealing both to your humanity and your Christian responsibility for the most vulnerable, to use your role as Leader of the House of Commons to ensure that even in these final days of this Parliament their cry for justice and compassion is finally heard.

It would be simply unforgiveable if those who experienced systemic abuse as children through institutions of the Church and State, should once again have their reasonable hopes for justice, care, compassion and basic human understanding frustrated by a further and totally unnecessary delay by the institutions of Government in Westminster. There is simply no other issue which deserves greater priority. I therefore appeal to you to make the passing of the NI HIAI Legislation Bill your highest priority when timetabling the legislative business of Westminster to be completed before the end of this term.

With every good wish,
Yours sincerely,

Fr. Timothy Bartlett
Administrator
St. Mary's Catholic Church
Chapel Lane
Belfast BT1 1JJ.

CHAPTER FIVE

Having once again just been released from yet another prison sentence, I concurred that my difficulties and haphazard lifestyle would likely continue because of not having a close family setting and home life. Due to being taken away from our close family home in our early years and having been separated as very young children, we had lost the natural sibling bonding that is usually ingrained into families, along with the inherent built-in attachment to one's parents. In our setup, the family bond was mainly broken and lost, particularly with our birth mother, who had decided to leave us.

My father had by this stage owned his house outright and was given the offer to sell it to the recently formed housing executive organisation, which had commenced a regeneration scheme. This was in the late 70s and early 80s as we, his children, had flown the nest in one way or another, all going our separate ways in life, even from each other.

The scheme had introduced a project of demolishing older houses, which desperately needed to be completely overhauled. Many houses already unfit to live in by modern standards were long overdue remedial aid, as in other sprawling areas in and on the outskirts of Belfast. Many people had declined entering the re-homing project hoping for greater remuneration, if they held back. That was indeed their entitlement to do so. They stayed in houses that may have been the only ones standing, adjacent to adjoining bricks and mortar of collapsed or collapsing gable walls. Others had been offered choices and new opportunities to settle in housing estates all over Northern Ireland. My father, who, after enquiring after me for quite a while, finally moved out and settled back into the country area in Co. Derry which he was from, before moving up to Belfast. He had concluded in his heart that I wouldn't ever come back or ever want to stay there again, perhaps realising I was now old enough to make my way in life. I feel the 'city', as he had called it, brought him too much pain, suffering, distress and problems. I now know that because he had to agree with the word of the Church and Welfare that we, his children, would be better placed into care, it broke his heart and mind. He tried his best to keep us out of care and to remain living with him. He worked and always held down a job. The authorities had said they would find us a more suitable place to live, but we now know how disastrous and untrue that was for us. My father suffered deep shame knowing we were in those awful institutions. He wanted us with him, and he did try to get us out most holiday times, or at least an odd weekend.

He took the four of us back in those days to his mother's house. Our granny in the countryside of Co. Derry where we would be met by his sisters and brothers, our aunts and uncles. Those times away from Nazareth were so precious. A taste of normality, a taste of freedom and peace, free from pain, as we ran around free as birds amidst the long stems of barley in fields adjacent to my granny, playing hide and seek in her haystacks at harvest time, eating cooked eels at the side of Lough Neagh, fried on a pan atop a primus stove. A taste of heaven mixed with apprehension come Sundays, knowing our time of freedom was ending, so akin to our last supper away, before being driven back to the dark despairing dungeon of the prison rooms in the care homes.

Our father showed us all parts of the countryside where he was born and reared, telling us stories of going to school barefoot across the fields and country lanes, with him having to walk a few miles there and back, even in the cold winters...they were good memories he told us, most probably because he was free. He married our mother late in life, she was much younger than him, and they moved to Belfast so he could get work. He liked to work and to keep himself busy. It was all he knew. He could put his hand to anything. He could fix cars with a self-learned expert knowledge beyond his natural skills. He always found a way through the mechanisms of oily and petrol-strewn engines of old cars and bicycles. That's when I recall he was happiest, always under the bonnet or undercarriage of a vehicle. Dad stored spare car parts and tyres in our backyard of all shapes and sizes, and many passers-by called to see if he could help them with car parts, which he so often did.

In my after-school years, as I always wanted to wander and to be elsewhere rather than the family home, it often brought me into the wrong type of company and a circle of fellow seemingly lost and lonely souls. I caught up with a few old contacts and resumed my fast-becoming familiar way of life, this after a short while of desperately not wanting to do so. Alas, it was a way of life for many back then. With no money, job, or nowhere to live, I fell into the usual old haunts and hangouts from before I went to jail.

Unfortunately, after one of these drunken brawls, I was arrested and charged with assault and duly sentenced to four months imprisonment in Armagh Jail once again. This occurred after a crowd of us had remained in the bars late into the night when another fight broke out in which I was stupidly involved. Police were called, charges were eventually pressed, and I was driven off in a prisoner transit van, brought to jail, and once again locked up in a prison cell. This time inside, many more political prisoners were on the remand wings because of the 'The Troubles,' which led to many people being arrested and thrown into jail, guilty or not guilty. Such were those torrid times with corruption, illegal cover-ups by agencies, clandestine shoot-to-kill policies and agendas to fill the prisons to take people off the streets as noted in several other books that have been published in recent years.

The jail was noticeably packed on all the floors. I could see this by scanning the various levels through the wire mesh that divided the landings. I was in a cell on the same ground floor as before, so I was familiar with the process and routine of the daily running of the prison system. As usual, and as I had done on my last visit to jail, I made a rough cut-out makeshift calendar to mark off the days until I would be free again, ticking off each day, hoping once again I would be free with a month's remission if I behaved. I was met with the usual familiar faces of the last time, which helped lessen the upset of my being locked up again. At least knowing some of the prisoners and the wardens helped me cope much better. Then came my release date, and I could leave my prison cell. As I left, I once again promised myself that this would be my last time in prison, and I meant it this time. I knew I would have to stop going to places I had frequented, but more so to stay away from my old ways and bad habits of hanging around the edges of the town centre, which only got me into big trouble.

Whilst in jail and after having been in and out a few times, I would, at times, cry myself to sleep after wishing and praying that my upbringing could have been different, and I could have had a normal childhood without having been placed into the convent with ungodly, uncaring nuns and priests. Always softly crying, my questioning within my wracked sobbing body...as to why no one was there to show genuine love and acceptance to me in this world. I was fed up with pretending I was a tough nut who didn't care about anyone or anything. I was done with acting and pretending I didn't care about getting into trouble. It was all a big laugh and nothing I couldn't handle; those were the lies I told myself! But, as always, when I got out of prison again and again, I had to put on my hardened exterior, my mask and protective armoured cloak. I had to face the big imperfect world again. I could never let anyone see me cry, as I had always wrongly thought crying was a weakness...(oh, how to the contrary, I now realise, how so very wrong I was).

On my release from jail, I changed my friends or, more so, my associates and tried to behave as an everyday citizen doing my best to stay out and away from trouble. This I did and settled down somewhat, doing what most of my new friends were doing and led a quieter life. I stayed with a married couple who were my friends in the university area, had a job to go to every day, with not needing to go near the city centre's old haunts and old ways of shoplifting again.

I made many friends who were either students at Queen's University or dropouts who had had enough of studying and preferred to bum around on wacky tobacco and other drugs going around at the time. I didn't take to smoking joints. The effect made me too quiet and paranoid depending on what company I was seated with. I always preferred a drink, whereby I could watch people and be on the alert. Such was my thinking at times, with heightened antenna signals sending warning signals against oncoming attacks.

I was paranoid most times, I'm sure because I had almost gotten used to these things happening from my early days of life in the care home. Things were quite good then. Parties happened often, and as usual, when I had too much alcohol taken, I sometimes shouted my mouth off, getting barred out of the local pubs for being disruptive. And, of course, never remembering what or why I had started or been involved in arguments for. Then, I always had to beg to get reinstated to the local pubs, much to my embarrassment. What made this happen and for what reasons, I, at the time, didn't know or realise. I recall people telling me I was lovely when sober or with a few drinks, but when I had too many, I was called 'hate the world.' This was when a fit of uncontrollable anger would erupt from within me, with my taking it out on any bystander who was near enough and whom I thought was talking about me or laughing at me. This 'lovely girl' would then turn into the Incredible Hulk.

Around that time, I met with my first serious boyfriend, whose family had moved to the Ormeau Road area from Carrick Hill in North Belfast. We became inseparable, going everywhere together, walking arm in arm, hand in hand to cinemas and parks, visiting his relatives, and announcing our togetherness to the world ever so proudly. After many years of a former lifestyle which was horrendous, I started doing the things that any normal young adult should be doing. I began to live a stable enough lifestyle going to the discos and nightclubs where I had met him. We had been going out with each other for a few years and had gotten the fun nicknames of Bonnie and Clyde on the road from those who had known him and me. He was renowned for being a hard man, a fighter who wouldn't back down, but underneath, he was very kind and gentle, just like me underneath that cloak of protection. I felt that because he had to live up to his reputation and this name placed upon him, he was never afraid to face up to anyone who confronted him. I think this often happens when you've got a name for yourself and one of being able to look out for yourself in street or bar brawls. This mainly happened in pubs and clubs, especially during the 'Troubles' when people were aligned with various sections of the community in the war-torn streets of Northern Ireland. Too much alcohol brought already heightened tensions to a higher degree. Some drunken people would come up and confront him. He wasn't on the lookout for fights; he was primarily drawn into the fight through the anger and rage of people provoking him deliberately, which would happen often. He had been in jail too, and Borstal was situated in the youth wing of Armagh Jail. Strange to find out that he had done time as a teenager in the very jail that I had previously been in as a teenager.

We stayed over in my long-time friend Big Joan's old house back on the Ormeau Road, which was a squat, squatters rights or not...being the law of the land or not...in those heady days of the early and late '70s. I had long forgotten my old ways of rioting and bonfire days and was discovering a new life of somewhat normality, even holding down a job that brought us both money for outings. The army raiding houses were quite a normal occurrence back then.

Suddenly, early one morning at around 4.00 am, the British army and police came banging on my friend Joan's house door. I assumed they wanted to arrest my long-time boyfriend, just as they had done in earlier years for minor anti-social behaviour. I immediately thought the army was there for him because of his past of petty criminal activities, but they arrested me! I was quite astonished when the army and special branch with them shouted it was me, they wanted and that I was under arrest under some section of the Terrorism Act.

Army Saracens had escorted special branch vehicles into the built-up area of rows of terraced houses, slamming heavy steel doors and noisy diesel engines, waking the neighbours up as they usually did on their quest to narrow the huge numbers of those who committed the crimes. Politicians spoke out daily on media news outlets demanding police should be locking up those who had carried out bombings and shootings that had occurred monthly if not weekly, in Northern Ireland, particularly in Belfast and its outskirts.

I was taken to Castlereagh Holding Centre and questioned by plain clothes detectives where they told me about the bombing of 'The Wimpy' bar restaurant in the town centre and alleged that I was involved in it. I was stunned at this accusation; they tried the good cop/bad cop you'd see on television crime series. I kept telling them I was not a bomber or involved with any paramilitary organisation. I believe they knew rightly that I was never involved with Republicans. Yes, I lit many bonfires years before and fought with them and the army and police at any stage I could with bricks and bottles...but this was way back in my early teenage years. I wasn't this person anymore. I was more mature and trying to grow up to be a law-abiding citizen.

So, the army came to arrest me and brought me to the holding station where all other terrorist bombers, killers, and both sides of the community had been held and interrogated. I felt they were now trying to frame me. The special branch of Northern Ireland framing me for something I certainly didn't do, nor ever would have. When I realised this wasn't a joke and that they were serious about charging me with this bomb attack, I got furious. I trashed up the cell, banging on the door and attempted to wreck the bedding area. The cheek of them trying to get me to sign a confession to admit that I blew up the bar restaurant with explosives when nothing was further from the truth. I shouted at the special branch woman, trying to lunge at her across the wooden table between us in the small interrogation, greyish-white-walled room. I was in shock, but I was aware of their covert attempts to entice me with the good cop/bad cop scenario. I thought that they were very immature and comical. If it wasn't so serious, I could've laughed at their behaviour as if I wasn't aware of what they were doing. They were trying to tell me that I did something that I knew wholeheartedly that I didn't do, that I wouldn't do, that I wasn't even around people who would have the material to do so. I never bothered with those people, so why they chose to arrest me, I'll never know. The army, MI5/6, arrested and charged so many innocent people throughout 'The Troubles', beating up and torturing hundreds, if not thousands, in the interrogation units, into signing statements of guilt, though not all were innocent.

So many people during 'The Troubles' went into jails and served long sentences even though they were not guilty. Such were the illegally used powers of the 'Special Powers Act' of the security forces. Many were forced under duress in the notorious Castlereagh Holding Centre to admit to doing something they didn't. I certainly was not going to do so. They didn't assault me or torture me. It was enough to be mentally tortured, laying in the cell thinking that they, the so-called 'law of the land', could send an innocent person to prison by setting them up just because they could. This was soul-destroying.

They held me there for three days whilst they attempted to tell me what I had done, when and how and with whom. I tried my best to remember where I was on those specific dates. Desperate to recall so far back, I wracked my brain into thinking just where I had been on those dates. I thought back day by day to try to recall exactly where I had been on those dates that they told me I had been in the restaurant, desperately trying so hard. They tried to tell me that I went into the Wimpy Bar, ordered a strawberry sundae, sat down with another woman, set down a bag and then left. And they wanted me, to tell them; 'yes, this was true.' They had not even written out a statement for me to sign. There was no pressure or the usual shouting or coercion, that one would see in the movies. I believe they did it just because they could. Ridiculous!

I was brought to Donegall Pass police station, where I was put in line with around eight or ten other women whom the police had called in from the streets around the Shaftsbury Square area, asking them to line up beside me so the alleged witness could pick out the arrested person amongst them. I knew then they were trying to frame me for this, but I still believed they would release me, as they had no evidence. I was innocent, and they knew it. I thought I was getting out the next day after the good cop/bad cop performance led to no statement being signed and my telling them what to do with it. Instead, they told me I would go before an identity parade, which I agreed to, telling myself I'd never get picked out and be freed.

I was placed in the middle of the identity parade. I seriously knew with all my heart that the person who was the so-called witness didn't look at me at all and was looking at the other people in the line-up. I was laughing inside about this ridiculous setup as the person who had come into the outer courtyard and who was supposed to be the witness ended up in such a nervous state she practically rushed off. Not once did she look towards me, and certainly did not pick me out, as she walked up and down nervously shaking her head, saying "no, no!".

A duty solicitor who was supposed to be on board to represent me at the sham parade, to look on as it happened, didn't seem to raise any issues about the lack of identity. I somehow still don't believe he was a genuine solicitor as he didn't speak up for me or argue that I wasn't picked out because they drove me to Town Hall Street police cells to stay overnight before my special appearance in court the following day. I wasn't clued into the knowledge of asking for certain solicitors who I could trust. I didn't know any, nor did I have contacts with anyone who was connected to paramilitary groupings to ask for advice. How could I then be suddenly charged, accused, and remanded in custody? Why and for what reason?

So, here I was up in court and remanded in custody again, sent on to Armagh Jail, only this time it wasn't for disorderly behaviour, assault or shoplifting. It was for my being falsely accused of allegedly bombing the Wimpy Bar Restaurant. This time on arrival at Armagh Prison, I was told to go upstairs to the Republican wing of the prison, where I was met by a few girls who asked me to make a statement. I laughed out loud, telling them I'd nothing to write about, only what had happened on my arrest, so this I did, a statement saying I have been framed, also telling them I am a former shoplifter, not a bomber, never was, never will be.

Though I was on the upper wing, I had my cell and told them I would stay away towards the far end of the wing and mix with other people who were in for minor incidents. I said I did not want to remain with them because I would not be imprisoned for a life sentence for something I didn't do. I told myself if I do, it's like admitting to doing the bombing. The prison officers and everyone else would feed back to the special branch that I was mixed up with the Republican struggle, and they, the special branch, would be happy enough with that, yet another off their 'false and made up' wanted list.

I knocked about with the ODCs, which means ordinary decent criminals. Yes, I preferred to be around these people! The person in the next-door cell to me was again another Loyalist involved in a murder. She said she

90

was innocent though whether she was or not, I didn't know. I wasn't going to be her judge and jury. She was from a notorious part of Portadown, and only in later years I realised she was a girlfriend of a well-known killer member who murdered many innocent Catholic citizens.

The girls from Sandy Row whom I had known from my previous terms in prison were still there, though not on remand, but now sentenced to many years for murder or involvement in attempted murder. They were locked up on the wing below me. I chatted with them regularly when I was allowed down to get hot water for tea or association times. I had told the older woman in charge of them, whom I had gotten to know quite well from my previous spells in prison, that I had nothing to do with the charges. They believed me and gathered I wasn't involved with any paramilitary grouping. They remembered me from my past prison sentences when I had served time for minor criminal activities.

Shortly after having been there a few days, I felt myself becoming very low with a sinking feeling of the terrible thoughts of being locked away for many years, never to see the outside for a very long time, asking myself how and why this could happen to me. In the meantime, I could only look forward to seeing my boyfriend and a few mates at visiting times. He couldn't believe what had happened to me either, knowing that we were always together. He knew I had never bothered or had connections with anyone of that ilk. I had once again made a makeshift paper calendar for my tiny cell wall, counting off the days that went by and marking them off one by one. Only this time, I had marked off more days and months than my earlier visits to the cells. This time, it was growing into the longest term spent in prison, with my calendar ticking off four 'full' months, with no sign of it ending anytime soon, nor with an end date to look forward to.

Meanwhile, some of the prison officers who had gotten to know me well from being in jail somehow knew that I wasn't involved and wasn't guilty of this charge against me. They thought back to the times when they used to laugh as I clowned about innocently, just like a child who had never grown up. On the other occasions I spent in jail, I was always fooling, joking and playing around many times getting into trouble, put on report and almost losing out on remission. Yet somewhere deep beneath, there was a broken-hearted little child who was hurting, but she couldn't just dare let anyone know or see that.

I remember one day; a medical orderly off-handedly asked me if it was alright if she wrote a letter on my behalf. I didn't understand what she meant by this, thinking it was to get me an excellent report to the Principal Officer in charge of the prison. I never took anyone so seriously as to think for one moment anyone would really, sincerely care about my situation. This warder helped with ailments and medicines, she was the doctor's assistant, and as she spoke to me about wanting to do this for me, I laughingly agreed. On thinking back, she and they had probably been talking about me at some stages at their weekly meetings, noticing that I wasn't in the paramilitary wing and that I didn't, nor hadn't, joined in with any of their meetings or activities. This warder was a decent Christian lady, a gentle soul, as she was often kind, pleasant and genuinely caring, evident in her medical practice. Usually, I prayed sincerely for someone like that to come along and see that I was innocently framed and set up, that someone would believe me, often crying out to God to help me get free from this place.

This pleading within me went on, praying that someone, somewhere, would know that I was innocent and help to release me from this prison cell. On many nightly occasions, my tears not only fell on my pillows but onto the floor. Always when the heavy steel door was tightly closed shut, then my tears would fall behind closed doors when alone. Perhaps God used her to do this for me because up to that time, I hadn't stopped asking God for help, crying in muffled tones... "please help me, God, you know I'm innocent, get me out of here". There was a local priest who used to visit remand prisoners now and again, in between his saying Mass on Sundays. As a matter of course, he asked me if I needed anything, and I half-jokingly said, "Yes, will you bring me up the prayer of St Jude of Hopeless Cases?" This he did. I held on to it daily and nightly, begging God to get me off with this case I was wrongly accused of.

I now mostly preferred to be alone on the wing, where I had a cell to myself this time. I befriended only a few who were on remand for a week or two, then released and out again. Such was the court system. I so often wished this would be me one day, though every week I travelled to the courts only to be remanded to prison again and again. I preferred to be kept separate in the prison van on weekly remand court days. I mostly sat at the end near the back door of the prison van, whilst other women who were also going to the remand courts in Belfast from Armagh sat near the driver's end. This was when my long-learned trait and coping mechanism kicked in, my humming to myself to ward off or muffle the sound of their sniggers and comments a few of them had sniped down towards me. Most were nice enough to me, though some thought they were big tough nuts, just doing it in front of the others. Most likely, when alone and with no audience to show off to, they too cried into their pillows, begging to get out of prison and to go home.

I had been wrongly imprisoned for four months, which seemed like four years, when I was summoned by a warder and told that the Chief Principal Officer wished to see me downstairs in her office. It was late evening when the PO told me to get ready and pack my bags for a special court sitting on a bank holiday at Belfast Courthouse the following morning. I was in shock, so I asked her why and what for, but she wouldn't tell me, she just said, "Margaret, just go pack your belongings". As I exited her office, my stomach knotted and heaved with anxiety and bewilderment. On passing the cell next door, the Sandy Row loyalist group leader called me in. I went into her and said I had been told to be in court the following day and pack my bags. She was delighted for me, telling me they all knew, as loyalist prisoners, that I was innocent. I was so excited but fearful, telling her I would not pack my bags as I would be so ashamed in front of people in the wings if I were to come back again carrying my bags of clothes. I just couldn't believe this was happening and that I was to go court and it was not my usual date. "What if, what if?"

Oh, my God, I couldn't sleep, but I prayed even more and asked God to please let me be set free from this prison. I was sick with nerves. Early the following day, I wore a beige three-piece suit for the occasion. I took nothing else with me, too embarrassed to think I would have to come back in again. Such was my disbelief that this might happen, that I may be actually set free.

When the prison officers were ready and waiting to take me out early the following day, I jumped into the van that speedily brought me to Belfast

Courthouse. The judge held up a document and read out an order deeming I should be released immediately, that the charges were being dropped as there was no evidence to substantiate my being held in custody any longer! I smiled in disbelief, now believing my prayers had been answered. I was indeed being set free. The judge released me and said the charges against me were no longer held up. I was innocent and wanted to thank the medical officer who wrote the letter. Somehow, on my behalf, I believe she was used by God. On release from the court, which was quite near the road and area where I was from, I skipped and ran from the courthouse, smiling from ear to ear through the market area, waving to people as I went telling them I was set free and running on up towards the Ormeau Road to my friend's Belle's house. She and her family squealed in delight to see me, staring at me in disbelief. Then both of us went up to my sister's house, where her husband went to look for my boyfriend. Suddenly, he was in my sister's house in no time, hugging me in surprise and amazed that I was free. I was so happy as we all celebrated my release. We celebrated for many weeks after that until I returned to earth with a bolt. The thoughts of that prison cell wouldn't leave me. I could have been in prison for twenty or more years for nothing. After being out of prison for a few weeks, realising what had happened and how it had hit me hard and affected me more than I thought it would, I went out more often, drinking to try to forget.

My relationship with that boyfriend fizzled out, and after a year or two of my release from jail, I decided I wanted to get away from Belfast entirely. I was invited to go to London with a few girls I had got to know and jumped at the chance, never having been there before. So, off we went to one of the girl's squats in London.

One evening, I got knocked down by a black taxi, which severely broke my femur in half, and I ended up in St Thomas' Hospital. My leg was held up on traction after a long steel pin was inserted the length of my thigh from my left hip to my knee. Such was the femur fracture's severity, that it was not mending naturally or correctly. I had various x-rays and a very extended stay of another four long months in London, locked up in the hospital. I was happy it was not another prison cell I was locked up in!

With plenty of time to think, I asked myself once again, as I probably may well have done so often. "Is this my lot in life?" Locked up as a three-year-old child in my early years, locked up again in my teens, late teens, early twenties and now my mid-twenties. Whatever was going to happen next in my eventful journey through life? Something just had to change, and I was determined this time it would. Time to find out who I was, who my mother was, if she was alive, and to find her, if only to satisfy myself that I was wanted at some stage of my early life. On to my next adventure and the journey of searching for and finally finding my birth mother.

CHAPTER SIX

The following years rolled by, and relationships and situations began coming to an end, fizzling out or simply changing course as is the natural transition in one's journey with the sudden realisation we have once again taken the wrong path in life or admitting to ourselves that we've come to the end of that particular chapter. In growing to maturity, we begin to learn from our mistakes and, hopefully, try once again to get back on the right road.

I was now treading carefully on my new path of life with my new family, my three young sons and with the sole desire and hope to give them the best start and plenty of what I didn't have in my own childhood. We were all in our new home together, with five years difference between the boys, knowing all I had was the instinct to do my best in looking after them and protecting them. After having my first son, I moved away from the area I was originally from and into another part of Belfast. Within the next ten years, I had another two sons, though I broke away from that relationship also, coming to an understanding that, in life such as it is, we often fall into relationships thinking and hoping they may last but they don't. Unfortunately, we often make wrong choices, finally coming to accept this and knowing it's best for everyone to move on.

I still felt something was missing in my life, although for a very long time, I ignored it until something began to stir up within me, making me question what I was still inadvertently searching for or missing. This feeling beneath my steel suit of protective armour, which began interrupting my thoughts, frightened me - disturbingly so. Was my heart beginning to soften? How could I dare to even think of 'her'? Would that be a betrayal of my long stance of pretending not to care, that she didn't matter in my life? Was it wrong to begin feeling the urge to find her? Would that be a weakness? Why was I, after all these years, now forty-three, with three beautiful sons yearning to find out if my birth mother was still alive or perhaps dead? I never really had her in my mind at all prior to this, totally blocking her memory from my thoughts.

A while after having had my first son and after my sister and I had a few drinks one particular night, I began, in a joking manner looking into phone books after finding out my mother's married name. Someone had told us both that she had married a brother of a man who lived nearby. We started looking at the yellow pages. It was easier to emphasise it that way for fear of further rejection. Well, it happened that her name was in the phone directory, but with a misspelt surname, I didn't find it and let it go completely.

Around fifteen years later, I knew the time was right to start the search, and I asked an official whom I trusted if she could help to find out about 'her' with the help of the Salvation Army. It came back a few months later that the search had come to a dead end, although I found out subsequently that wasn't truly the case. I then decided to do my own investigation. I contacted the adoption society and other places, who said it would be very hard to find her, especially if she didn't want to be found. The woman I spoke with tried to put me off making enquiries about her, and I wondered why. I began finding out pieces of information along the way. I was by that time determined to prove them wrong, telling myself I darn well would continue and I would find out about her, one way or the other.

I was now on a mission. As I wholeheartedly went about this and was now open and no longer fearful of interacting with those who may have known her from the past, I was told she had another family. Taken aback, I carried on with fierce inner strength. I was informed that her first child had also been placed into St Joseph's Nursery of Nazareth Lodge as a young baby, having been seen on the grounds of Nazareth Lodge a few years after we had been placed into the same institutions. That made me very upset hearing this, and I then decided to find the children if I could instead of searching for her. Such was my dismay and hurt.

Earlier, I had gone to the Department of Deaths, Births and Marriages in Belfast city centre and paid for a search to run her name through their records. It took a little while, and unexpectedly I received a letter telling me they had copies of some information that may help me. I was able to retrieve the marriage certificate of my parents, and it was only then I realised how young she was compared to my father when they had married. Seeing the dates of birth on the documents I was given, my heart mellowed a little as I felt more compassion for her and perhaps some sympathy. It gave the former addresses of our first family homes in the Saintfield Road area and upper Ormeau Road and where we were baptised and by whom. This information was so precious to me as I hadn't known any of this.

It was indeed the opening of a Pandora's Box full of secrets pouring out. It was becoming strangely exciting delving into something it seemed that no one else had fully known, only me. I decided, by chance, to phone up St Joseph's Nursery Home and spoke to a lady who worked there who asked me for my name and what the query was. Unbeknownst to me at the time, the lady in question knew me very well, and I knew her and her family from my teenage years.

I had never spoken of this before to anyone at all, so no one knew of my history. No one. I couldn't dare to allow anybody to know of my shameful past and secrets. A miracle happened that day, and throughout the following weeks, the lady who knew me was able to find out information about my mother. Still, much more interesting than that, a massive breakthrough was about to happen...Pandora's Box had opened much wider. The lady, with a helpful nun by her side, had phoned me back that week, and they both gave me my birth mother's phone number, her address and other information on her children.

Up to that time, I had a file opened with pieces of information I had gathered, all packed securely into it. The file included a scrap of paper that a nun from Nazareth House, which was further up the road, had given me a week or so earlier after I had very hesitantly and, with a deep fear, phoned them to ask if I could call in just to chat.

As I walked up to the building with a friend who constantly reassured me as we neared the door, she noticed I was in shock and total disbelief that I had been allowed to go in and that this was really happening after all these years. The nun beckoned us in and with my friend doing all the small talk, she showed us the newly decorated dormitories where I had been once placed, now recently partitioned into small cubicles with more privacy. Noticeably, it had changed so much on the inside, with more modern brighter bedding and sitting rooms which now housed both boys and girls. This change happened because they now received much more money from the government, which they eventually allowed to oversee the running of the institution.

I began to feel overwhelmed and only wanted to get out of it quickly. I had seen enough. I hurriedly asked what information she may have on us, not knowing what, if anything, she may have. She opened a large ledger near the front door, and with a torn corner of a page she had ripped off from a holy reading book, she hurriedly scribbled down the dates of our admissions on being taken into their care, our dates of birth and our parents' names. That was it, a yellowed fragment of an age-old corner page, and this held all we had to show of our childhood lives, handed to me on a small piece of scrap paper.

I held onto this as I almost ran out of the building, thankfully knowing I would never be back in it again as long as it stayed standing. As we walked out onto the road, I nervously looked back at it, observing from the outside that it was still a terrifying old, darkened red, bricked building, surrounded by tall, dark leafy trees from which the sun never shone through into the inside, even on high peak summer months. In my still-childhood mind and machination, it would remain forever with me of what it looked like back then, along with the same terrifying memories which still remain and will forever. The encapsulated screenshot of a cold and haunted like demesne, likened to the darkened dungeons of Dracula's Castle, soulless, loveless and lifeless, is the true likeness and always will be in a child's mind, in my mind now even as an adult. Newly painted and decorated insides would never take or hide away the truth that had witnessed so many secrets and of shameful acts that fell upon innocent children behind those high walls, walls which kept us all mainly hidden from the outside world for many years.

Back in the safety of my home with my children, I opened my secret file to read through what information I had stored up until now as the treasured cache of my earlier life as a child was beginning to be revealed. I somehow began to trust that something, along with someone, was going to be presented to me very soon if I dared to keep believing. No one got to see my file. It was placed under my pillow in bed at night and went everywhere with me during the day, always under close protection and never out of my sight. This folder held many secrets, and now that I had the phone number and address of my birth mother, I felt it was time to travel up to where she lived.

I exited my car and started the long walk down her street. Passing by her window with a friend standing tall beside me to block me, in case she was able to see me looking in at her, I tried to catch sight of her. I did this on a few occasions, firstly hoping she would appear, and one day she eventually did. She was sitting on her couch directly facing the front window. My stomach was in knots, my heart fluttered wildly, and I felt I was on a top-secret mission, and I suppose you could call it just that. It was indeed my big secret. I didn't dare tell many as it was too early to do so. I wanted to know if she was alive, but more so, I needed to find out if she would speak to me or wanted to know me at all.

My next plan of action was to phone the house, which I did if only to hear her voice. Then, I would put the phone down, saying sorry wrong number and ring off quickly. One day, I decided to ring up for real, praying she wouldn't put the phone down on me. I rang her number, and she answered. As I knew her voice by then, she asked who I was, and I gave her my name, which confused her momentarily. I told her not to be shocked and that I didn't wish her any animosity at all, that I just wanted to contact her. I told her I understood if she didn't want to bother, that would be fine too, though inside I didn't want that at all. I heard her choke up a little, obviously in shock

100

and suggested she get a drink of water or something and that everything was going to be alright. I was more concerned for her well-being than my own. I found out later that she ran to the kitchen cupboards, grabbed the first bottle she could see and swigged down a gulp of whiskey. She asked me my name again. I'm not sure if she had forgotten or had done what I had done; in pushing all the memories of us to the back of her mind, maybe she was still in deep shock? She settled a little as I spoke softly to her, reassuring her and taking time to make light of the situation.

I asked her the names of her children and their ages, which I scribbled down on sheets of paper within my secret folder. The ease with which I did this and the breakthrough of it happening had to be, indeed, yet another miracle and an answer to my prayers. I had been praying out to God, for a very long time now, from my times in the prisons and in the docks of courtrooms, that if God would help me, I would turn my life around with His help. I do believe this is what was now happening. Doors were opening left, right and centre. I told her all about my children, my sister and two brothers. I chatted away freely without judgement or condemnation and with a finality of forgiveness. I told her I didn't hold anything against her, that I understood things happen in life and there are always two sides to a story, two people and that I wasn't interested in the 'who-did-whats-and-whys' anymore.

After speaking for quite a while, I left things with her saying if she wanted to meet up, she could call me back and that we would like to meet her new family. Saying our goodbyes, we then both hung up. I was walking in a daze, asking myself, 'What had just happened? Is this for real? Am I imagining things?' I giggled like a child, feeling so happy, amazed, though totally bewildered, at the same time.

The phone rang the next day, and she spoke more openly then, agreeing to meet up with us, saying she would bring one of her sons and her daughter, arranging to meet in a hotel near Lisburn. I rang my brother, having earlier rung my sister that day, and they were both in deep shock, but I was flying high with adrenalin. We met up as agreed. My sister and a friend arrived early, choosing a private booth in a corner of the hotel.

Then we saw her walk in. I think earlier on the phone, we had given a description of ourselves which made it easier to spot each other, though she didn't know that I had already got sight of her through her window. I didn't want her to be embarrassed in any way. I made sure it wasn't going to be a showdown of sorts but rather a friendly reconnection, and hopefully, all would go well from that. I paved the way somewhat for her, having said to my brother and sister that we didn't know the factual story of her own situation. Nor did we know the specific circumstances surrounding why she left the family home, and that now I knew she was so much younger she probably had her own problems in life, as many couples do. I had forgiven her. It wouldn't have worked out in this cordial manner many years ago. Even though I had assumed I had blocked her completely out of my mind, I now know I had held deep unforgiveness and umbrage towards her. I now realised I had never grieved for her after her leaving us.

On getting to know our birth mother, she wanted us to call her by her first name, as she knew it was difficult to call her 'mother' or 'mammy', not that we did or could. We began meeting up regularly. I felt a massive chip being removed from my shoulders; the weight that I carried was subsiding somewhat, even if a little, though it would take much longer to be healed entirely. I began to change inwardly and outwardly, feeling better about myself. Although there still seemed to be a deep wound of sadness remaining which sprang up every so often. I wouldn't find out why until many years later.

After a few years of getting to know our birth mother, we kind of grew apart. My sister had stopped taking her calls first. I believe she found it much harder to forgive, with her being five years older than me and having spent much more time with her in the family unit. I realise now that I had only forgiven her from a mature adult perspective, but the inner child within me had not. In the years ahead, I could finally do this through prayer. I was definitely happy enough just to have found, seen, known and spent time with her for those few years, and it did help.

My brothers were happy to have met her also, as it gave them some respite in their lives and healing from rejection even if only a little. She gave me a small package of photographs of us all as young children before being placed into care—those photographs I treasured. I got them enlarged and shared them with my two brothers and sister. These pictures were a blessing to have, something that showed us a little of our past life, in our childhood home together, sitting in front of our car, on bicycles, playing as a family, holding on to each other and our pets and toys in the garden. This made it feel real and helped us believe that, yes, we had a proper family at one stage of our early stages in life. Yes, we did, if only for so many years.

I believe that after finding out who my mother was, where she was and what she looked like (a lot like myself) and having met her, this was the beginning of my wholehearted decision to seriously want and desire to change my life - this new period of my life had lifted such a heavy load from me. I didn't have to pretend to myself that I didn't care about her, that it wasn't an issue anymore. I had found her and dealt with my negative thinking of her. I replaced those thoughts with the truth. Whilst doing so, I had now released a lot of misgivings in me and felt much freer and unburdened. I wasn't expecting at all to have a happy family life experience. I knew in my heart of hearts that if I met her, that would be enough in itself. After meeting with our birth mother, I quickly removed a few layers of the hardened shell of my protective covering.

As I had touched on earlier in this book, stating that many relationships often come to an end, I began to think to myself, was this always the case in my own life? Was there some mechanism in me that I now assumed they were always going to end?

Nevertheless, I believed meeting my mother was just the first stage in my recovery and that there were many more to go through in the future. After this breakthrough, I went to the library to study and read up on topics of psychology and how our thought patterns of either being positive or negative affected our daily moods and our daily living, with either ourselves or with those around us. I was now definitely on the right path in trying to find out about this, and I knew I must continue to do it.

To begin understanding what was wrong with me, why my behaviour was so out of control and why I hated myself so much, distrusted others, and was so anti-authoritarian, I began to re-educate myself and to gain a better, more objective understanding of my situation.

When I started reading up on self-help books, mainly by American author Louise Hay, I began finding out that the mind was a powerful tool for making me believe and act out that whatever I allowed into my thoughts, that was where they stayed and festered and played out my future. This, of course, produced and manifested into a parody of whom I believed I was, manufactured by the thoughts and beliefs I had of myself! Paragraphs in the book advised I should begin to speak out loud to myself, even though my embarrassment of doing so attempted to hold me back. I continued doing what I had learned from the books...telling myself that I was worthy, I was wanted and I was loved. I found it very hard and strange to attempt this, but I was so determined to do anything at all that would help me change my life. I felt, in a way, that I was fighting for my survival.

I had already started attending various courses in the local library that my neighbour had asked me to go along to. Then, we went to aromatherapy and relaxation classes in the local primary school that our children attended close by. I felt quite awkward doing this amongst others, exposing my vulnerability in front of them, it wasn't what or who I was...but I wanted to find out just who I really, genuinely was, so I forced myself to mix with the others. I was a very slow starter at first, hiding behind my mask, my exterior shield of protection, my hardened outer shell, which I'd created over many years. Slowly it was beginning to soften, to crack open.

Between attending these classes and getting to know others, I was shown that they, too, had problems, issues and vulnerabilities. I wasn't alone. I wasn't the only person in the world who felt the way I did. Knowing this allowed me to feel more comfortable in myself. I was kind of happy or reassured in a way that these others I had met in the classes hadn't got it all together either. I wasn't alone or the only one anymore, as I had thought, which made me smile again. I began to warm up and couldn't wait for the following classes, whether it was aromatherapy, reflexology, relaxation classes etc. I yearned deep inside to warm up this cold house in my head and heart that had imprisoned me, allowing me to be released from my insecurities and to be renewed in my body, soul and spirit. I was coming alive again, but it was at a very slow pace.

I recall the reflexology teacher massaged my feet, and on examination of them, she could tell me I was very vulnerable...I didn't know at that time what that meant! Even allowing her to touch my feet and massage them was a big deal for me as I didn't allow anyone to come that close to me and she was a stranger. We had to sit in a circle at the aromatherapy classes. We were told to close our eyes, breathe slowly, relax and imagine these beautiful memories and faraway places to help calm us. I had no pleasant memories or beautiful visions of holidays or mountain tops with sea-view cottages, but I suddenly recalled my granny's country cottage. So, I instead envisaged sheep on a green grassy slope, thinking of her little chickens running free, running through fields, and me roaming beside the river close by. This I did with my eyes opened wide; I wasn't ready to close them just yet.

I was often tempted to up and leave these classes so many times as I struggled so hard. I was very anxious and easily distracted and just couldn't concentrate or relax. I didn't know how to. I couldn't breathe properly, and many times in the early days of this, I felt feelings arise that I didn't understand or could hardly cope with. But I kept at it. I had no other choice. I had nothing better to do and didn't want to go back to my other ways of living, which led me into trouble.

Around this time, I also joined a small fellowship group on the road nearby. I needed a miracle. I was a hopeless case, I believed, as in the St. Jude prayer hopeless! And so, instead of going to our local Catholic Church, I joined this newly formed fellowship, which was a non-denominational grouping of people who were searching for meaning or/and change in their lives. I knew this was indeed a Godsend, a lifeline for me and if I were serious about wanting to change my life, I would try anything. The group ran an Alpha Course which had been running all over the U.K. and Ireland, north and south. This entailed finding out who God was. Was He real? how did He come about? What was He on earth for? how we came about, and to strengthen our faith if that was what any of us wanted. I already knew, deep down, that someone had intervened in my life that day in the courtroom, and I wanted to learn more about His miracles, kindness and forgiveness.

It was a mixed collection of individuals who were curious and wanted to find out more and also how others in the group had seen a turnaround in their lives. Those who had been there much longer and whose lives were already changed by these courses gave testimonies of their transformation to encourage us. I met some folk there who spoke openly of their pasts, their childhoods, their inappropriate relationships and incidents with the police and their times in prison!

Again, I was over the moon to hear this. I was rejoicing even then that there were many other people like me, and their lives were being changed. 'Miracles can happen', they said. I urgently needed one. 'Can it seriously happen to me?' I thought to myself. I was willing to go there to take part as there was nothing else in this life that I needed or wanted. I hungrily wanted what some of the others had peace of mind, body, soul and spirit. Soon after going to many of the Alpha Course meetings, I was getting prayed for and over. I wasn't used to this and had never seen it happen. Still, I craved desperately to be changed and that whatever was holding me back and destroying me in life be removed within me.

I recall us all sitting around and everyone closing their eyes in contemplation. I was the only one who kept my eyes wide open, always aware of who may be looking at me, perhaps mocking or smirking at me. It was quite a while into my Alpha Courses, of which I did so many, that I finally gained just a little confidence and some trust, or perhaps a letting go of what others might think, do, or say. I then somewhat relaxed and did it for me, me alone, only trusting in the One who would give me a new start in life, a new beginning finding that HE would be the one who genuinely cared for me, with no condemnation, without expectations or wanting anything in return! I read through the psalms constantly, unsure of their meaning at first, then gradually warming to them as they opened up in revelation before me, feeding me with truth as I carried on in my journey.

My mind began to be renewed by listening to the truth of who I was, who I was meant to be, and who I could become. I had to believe in myself. I had to have faith and trust that good things could happen to me and that I must stop telling myself that only bad things could happen to me. I had to thoroughly go through an operation of sorts, changing my wrong thinking, renewing my mind, believing that I was made good and worthy, that I was loved and lovable, that I was liked, that I had friends who wouldn't hurt me or abuse me, that I could learn to trust again, and that miracles do happen. I believed, and I received...my miracles.

After quite a few years of going to the fellowship, I was slowly growing into whom I *should* have been, but because of the damage and trauma that I'd suffered in childhood in Nazareth House, I had to be reprogrammed and to have the truth spoken over and upon me. I had to replace the lies and the wrong thinking patterns that had been embedded in me, by the daily name-calling, put-downs, spiritual abuse, wrong teaching, abusive humiliation with severe beatings and the constant verbal accusations spoken over me daily over the eight years of my being inside the cold, harsh and abusive institution.

Years of abusive background situations had to be brought up again, so I could be released from it, stuff that I was holding inside, secrets that I'd never revealed to anyone, many abusive situations that I'd gone through and endured alone because I had no one to fend for me, no one to look out for me.

It seemed everyone had left me to the might and power, and control of my abusers. But now, I was going to be changed and transformed. I believed it was happening as new doors began to open before my eyes. Miracles began to happen, which wouldn't have if it was solely left up to myself. This was only the beginning. I felt the prompting to go back to college and do my exams. I did various courses and exams and passed them all. I also discovered I could do well and thoroughly enjoyed creative writing, poetry and making flower arrangements. I was learning more about myself and my capabilities in various things. I realised I loved to write; I love the dictionary, spelling, adjectives etc. I got distinctions in Word and Text Exams and did ECDL courses. I excelled in English, earning an A star plus + for Oral Speaking - this I did in front of an entire class of students. I was astounded, as I didn't realise my potential until I began genuinely believing in myself, gaining confidence and telling myself I was capable of doing so.

After I completed my first-ever Curriculum Vitae, I was encouraged to send it to prospective job advertisers. A friend mentioned a position in a school who were looking for a junior admin. Her friend, who had already worked there for many years and said she would set up an interview for me. I was so nervous and began to doubt myself again, saying, what if they don't want me or like me? What if? I was sick with nervous exhaustion and couldn't sleep thinking about me going into a proper job, even as a junior admin.

My only and perpetual fear was Rejection! With a capital R. The time came around for the interview and I was accepted and started immediately the next day. I was overjoyed with excitement and with uncertainty at the same time. "Will it last? Nothing ever lasted in my life before this," I said to myself. Then, I heard a soft small gentle voice, "This time it's different, it's going to be ok. I will look after you. I will open doors for you that no one can open. If you continue to walk in my ways, I will watch over you and protect you. You are not alone; never again will you be on your own". I snapped out of my old ways of thinking and got ready for work.

I started in the office with Mary. She was a beautiful lady, kind and very gently spoken, who encouraged me to help her with anything she needed sorted, and I was so willing to put my hand to anything. I wanted to prove that I was and could be a nice person. I loved to help people out. I was stepping out into a new place, a new start with people. I was trying my best to trust them and hoped that they would trust me back. I enjoyed working in the primary school, (my youngest son was a pupil there also) and he was so proud to have his mummy working close by him. I often helped in the schoolyard as the children were on their breaks when they would come up to me calling out "Miss, Miss!"...wow, how times are changing; I smiled to myself, wondering what on earth was beginning to happen in my life, that I was being taken seriously and treated with respect.

The examinations were being conducted at this time, preparing for the main eleven plus exam. I was asked if I could fit in as a teacher, as one was off sick. I only had to supervise the children and make sure they kept behaving in an orderly manner. I sat at the top table looking around at them, young children about to head to secondary school. I felt very proud that I was there and trusted to look after them. They fully respected me, and I respected them, often joking with them. As I sat reading my own books, building my own faith and teaching myself how to look forward, not back and how to forgive my enemies, I was taken back to how my last years at primary school were very harsh and lonely, with no one to genuinely care for our schooling and our further education. I sincerely hoped these children would make it in the future and that they would never be lonely or hurt in their little lives now or in their futures.

After having been in the employment at the primary school for around a few months or so, Mary in the main office informed me the School Principal wanted a word with me. I had forgotten, at the time, that due to my working closely around children that they would ask for any police records in case I was a danger to the children, and rightfully so. The principal and I had gotten along very well. She was delighted to have me on board and often told Mary how glad she was to have someone who would do anything at all asked of her. As I arrived at the principal's office, she looked strangely at me as I entered through her door...she told me she had received the records and had some reservations now because on my records were a few misdemeanours that perhaps wouldn't look good if the board had caught sight of them! She was on the board also of the Catholic maintained school society and taught religion at the primary school. Well, I was shocked and hurt a little, but something came over me. The shock turned to a confidence that came from deep inside, as I said to her "My past is my past, I have been forgiven by the person who matters most in this world. If He has forgiven me, why cannot you?" She was astounded by my boldness in speaking up for myself. This was done not in my former aggressive attitude but in a newly found manner of self-respect and with an assurance that I was no longer living a life of guilt but had been given a new life free of condemnation! I'm not sure she understood fully, but as I left the room, I heard her say, "You have made me think about my own faith now. I should be showing forgiveness to you... I don't want you to have to go but let me see what can be done".

I was shattered on leaving but held on to my faith that this was not the end but only the beginning. Luckily for me, I'd already made an appointment to meet a friend to go to the cinema that night, and it helped take my mind off what had just happened. I kept telling myself, it's going to be okay; this time it's different. No one is rejecting you. This will turn out for your good; I kept quoting scripture and believing that something good was going to happen and not to worry.

I was told by my colleague and friend Anne that the religious teacher and Head Principal of the primary school had phoned non-stop that day and had persuaded a placement scheme worker to take me on as a junior admin, in a community project nearby. Reluctantly the woman who helped run the scheme gave in, and I started there. I knew that this was all a testing process for me, one to teach me how to be patient and how to interact in difficult situations and with difficult people without me getting angry, taking offence, or storming off, as was my former method in resolving situations. It wasn't a very productive place to be in. I wasn't given much to do but just retype a one-page document repeatedly. Joe, the project manager of this place was always very kind and pleasant to me, and that helped, though he was in an office on down the hallway out of the way from the main open plan area where I was seated. His daughter Marie Louise was often in and out, and Joe would introduce me to her. She works as a top health correspondent with BBC NI at present. It was like I was on a trial basis once again, I was bored, with having nothing to do each day, unless Joe politely asked me to help with his calls and other memos. I could either run away or stay and be determined to stick it out for the six months. Around four or five months into this placement, a new welfare and support officer for the surrounding area came in to provide services to the community, she and a youth leader, immediately connected with me and asked me to help and assist them in their work as community leaders, which I readily did, this making my time go by much quicker.

Then I was off, finished with my reprogramming, testing and yet another trial and ready for the next one in which, if I was serious about wanting to let go of my old attitudes, I had to go through. Whatever the tests and trials that had been set before me, I had no other choice at all but to keep moving forward and go through the fires, as it were. I desperately wanted to change my life at any cost to my 'pride' and devil-may-care attitude! This was why I allowed myself to come through certain humiliating instances whilst being there...without reacting or retaliating, thank God I didn't!

In the meantime, as proof of my genuine sincerity on wanting to be rid of my past and to change my ways, I updated my C.V. whilst I continued studying other subjects in further education, I was applying for any course to improve my chances of getting a job. This was more so to prove to myself I was capable and intelligent enough to take exams and to pass them, such was my newly found confidence and belief in my new self.

One morning after leaving my son to school, I noticed an advert on a window in an estate agent, advertising for an admin, person. This was located at the corner of the road where I lived at that time. I was told there were many in for the post, but I applied for it anyway, not really thinking I would succeed. The interview was very informal. I was quite relaxed and confident enough with my new C.V. in front of us on the table. The manager and I got on very well. No overpowering egotistical power-hungry boss to get along with, I thought, great. I got this job immediately. I knew the mental training in these places was a precursor to bringing me into line, to learn from volatile situations and how to react positively, just as I had to learn upfront from being in the past two admin, posts, and this to teach me how to cope face to face in difficulties, apart from my former ways of reacting, it wasn't easy...and this post was to be yet another one.

I worked in the Estate Agency business for two years, which taught me a lot, and I really enjoyed the experience. I got stuck into anything, learning from scratch, looking after the office, its clients, and wanting to help others whenever possible. I was often left in the office by myself to manage the offices. I had the keys to open and lock up the premises almost on a daily basis. I particularly enjoyed answering the phone, updating prospective buyers on their mortgages etc., getting to know the clients and managing how to deal with all folks in various situations. A learning game, I was learning a different way of behaving from the wrong ways I had picked up. I was teaching myself another way and manner of behaving rather than what I had in my previous attitude and defence mechanisms which usually went haywire. So, I was improving myself and learning, always in at the deep end, re-educating myself on how to react and what I could and couldn't do, especially under pressure and in heightened, volatile and extreme circumstances which occurred at times with customers! I was being stretched!!

After the two years of my employment came to an end because of the business closing down and the owner moving on to another adventure. I went out the doors for the last time, and I remember saying out loud, 'Oh Lord, where to now, what's next at this stage of my life, when will my next test and trial take place and where?' I had a feeling the next job I was to be employed in was to be the start of yet another very important venture into the full healing and more complete understanding of what had taken place to date in my life, and that vindication was very close to becoming a reality. This next stage, or chapter in my life, was to be the Beginning of the End.

CHAPTER SEVEN

Shortly after leaving my last job at the Estate Agents, I found a new position in a hostel. This came about also with the help of the same friends Anne and Brian. I had met Anne in the fellowship I attended, it was she who had put my name forward for the post as a junior admin assistant at the primary school also several years back. I recall repeatedly telling her I couldn't possibly be accepted to do this job, especially after what happened in the school. I once again thought they might think I was not good enough, or once they heard of my having a previous police record, they would reject me. My mind began to go haywire with stress and anxiety as the day neared the interview, so here I was, knowing I had to try it, or else I would give up on all things in trying to improve my life. I just had to fight off my insecurities and believe what Anne and Brian were telling me, that I had excellent social skills and a bright engaging personality.

That morning, I hesitantly but with a somewhat newly regained confidence and determination, strolled through the large, opened gates and across the treelined forecourt, now with almost a skip in my step.

I rang the bell, which instantly let me in. Walking through the open door, I met the manager in the hallway and realised we both had known each other from taking our ECDL/Computer Course exams in the same Community House of Further Education. With him already seemingly knowing me and that I had worked in the school and a Placement Scheme organisation after that, he assumed I would have been previously criminally vetted whilst working in my past jobs, and they took me on immediately. I honestly tried to tell him I had a minor petty criminal record from many years ago, but nothing would interfere with my working on these premises. He and others accepted me openly for who I was now and not what may have happened so many years in my past. Another open door with many blessings, it seemed. I believed my prayers were being answered, as this was yet another chance to continue turning my life around. I left the office with my head held high, smiling with renewed hope and a bigger spring in my step. I immediately went to my friend's house with the good news, my start date and a printed-out rota, with us both wondering where this new road would lead me to next.

Six months into working there, I began hearing various news items quite regularly relating to clerical abuse and the Ryan Report. These were inquiries and investigations involving children abused by church figures and those abused in religious-run institutions and training schools. At this time, the investigations leading to inquiries covered so many cases of clerical abuse in the South of Ireland.

I tried hard not to listen, thinking all this couldn't have happened and half of these horrendous stories must have been exaggerated. I had deliberately closed my mind and suppressed anything that had occurred in Nazareth House. As I tried to figure this out, I wondered how my denials had impacted me, especially as I was now openly hearing some of these reports, some so familiar, like those I had kept hidden. I knew in my heart that they were true. I now felt I would discover the truth about why I had been the way I was. As I wrote in an earlier part of this book, when stuff came up, I established a learned behaviour of how to force pain and triggers to dissipate and hopefully disappear, humming them away as in a mantra-type meditation. It worked for a while...though now, on hearing these reports, they were trying to catch my attention. Something, or someone, wouldn't allow me to ignore them anymore. At first, on hearing these reports, I could turn the radio or tv off, but now it was always front-page news in daily newspapers, right in front of my face, everywhere I went, almost demanding that I should stop, look and listen. I found it very hard to hear former residents of these institutions speaking of the brutality, rape, beatings, humiliation, and neglect they said was visited upon them by holy church figures and religious orders.

My head was completely messed up. I couldn't believe what I was hearing, as I always blamed myself for being the 'bad person', the 'problem child'. It was my fault and no one else's. I, alone, was the reason all these things happened to me in care and afterwards, not the religious order's fault.

In my new workplace, a small group of community nuns worked alongside me, and this didn't bother me at all. These few nuns wore civilian clothing and had been employed in the hostel from its early days throughout The 'Troubles' when it was once a women's shelter. I got on with them all. Many came up and down from Dublin to Belfast regularly and were involved with the church, so this didn't affect me in the least as I had my relationship with God, my faith and my beliefs.

One nun stayed overnight in her apartment and was a big part of the community where the hostel was situated and very close to where I lived at that time. We got along very well together. I enjoyed doing the gardens for her also, planting shrubs and filling flowerbeds, which pleased her so much, as they were her pride and joy. She and the other nuns had an accent that I began to suddenly notice after a few months into my post. Accents had only recently begun to trigger me, reminding me of sounds and echoes from the long ago past. I wasn't sure what or why this was happening or what was awakening within me.

One evening as I sat in the office, I began staring through the large clear glass window. I watched the tall trees blowing in the wind, noticing the shapes and shadows that eerily bounced off the red brick walls that circled the forecourt directly before me. Something began to resonate within me, akin to past images of my childhood that I had tried to blank out. Pictures and memories were suddenly coming back to my mind. Something was beginning to crack open in the deepest parts of my psyche, the hidden place. This was now visibly coming back up into the light.

My eyes filled with tears, and I cried sorely and heavily. On hearing my cries, I tried hard to stifle the sudden outburst of deep-seated grief rising from within. Somehow it brought me back to some of those awful years of Nazareth House, with my vivid imaginations of being right there and behind those red-bricked walls again. Flashbacks began rapidly, bringing me back in time with the same images I now watched from the window. I was suddenly propelled back to my childhood in care. I couldn't explain what was happening to me right then, but the floodgates were now opening wide. An outpouring of revelation was about to take place very soon. Attempting to compose myself as my late evening/night shift ended, I walked out towards the front door, eagerly handing over duty to my fellow worker who had just arrived to continue with all-night cover. I hurriedly gave him the keys, trying to hide my still noticeably reddened face after my tearful episode, said my goodnights, and somehow knew it wouldn't be long before I said goodbye.

The more I heard or caught sight of these news items, even unintentionally, the more I began to feel the emotional pain and trauma of the past. A while after this had been going on, I caught by chance or perhaps intentionally meant to be, an item on the BBC NI news at 6.30pm which shocked me. I watched as a man and woman spoke about their time spent as young children in the care of the same institutions my siblings and I had been in all those years ago. Somehow, I knew I was meant to hear this as they spoke about the various ranges of abuse and neglect, they went through as children. This made me finally realise they were discussing everyday things in the same institution. I was horrified, hearing what they said and what they went through, as this was similar to us, and it only awakened and stirred up other memories and horrors of yesteryear.

The severe harshness of the regime, the brutality, and the physical and sexual abuse of young boys made me feel sick. I instantly thought about my brothers and wondered what had happened to them, if anything. I didn't dare to believe so, though something began to play on my mind regarding one of my brothers. The man spoke of his time with the Christian Brothers, where my two brothers had been. I often wondered why this was the case, not knowing how or why he had been placed into a psychiatric home so soon after being released from the church-run institutions. These long unanswered questions in my mind about my brother and us all were quickly revealed as I delved further into what I had just heard! I prayed almost every night for all my siblings and my younger brother, who is presently in a nursing home.

I just knew right then that I had to contact this woman and man, a sister and brother, who were speaking out on television. I had instantly remembered her from many, many years ago, as my mind began to declutter and open. I phoned my sister and told her what I had just seen and listened to on local BBC NI television. She immediately agreed to pop into the nearby studios, nearby to where she lived. She asked that my contact details be given to the programme's producer with a request that we could speak and hopefully meet with the people who had just spoken out on tv.

Very soon after, my number was given over to the people who did the interview, contact was established, and after chatting a few times, we then arranged to meet up, where we both talked about the past. As we spoke, I noticed many more of my once-hidden memories gradually come to the fore, allowing me to look back in disbelief at the years I'd spent in the same place as this woman. She agreed to come back to Belfast again a few times, flying from England and bringing scanned photos with her, which I was in. One of the photos showed little girls standing in line for a staged photoshoot.

It broke my heart to see myself in the middle row of very young babies, mostly aged from three to five years old, standing with ragged dresses, straggled hair, with tears in their eyes, and there was myself, a bewildered, young three-year-old, looking like she wanted to run away and refusing to look at the camera. I burst into tears after seeing that little girl. I wanted to cuddle her, lift her out of that row of a very sad and tearful bunch of parentless babies. My heart ached for that very young child with no family members around her anymore. She was no longer in her own family home but now was standing in a cold grey forecourt surrounded by high walls and tall trees, locked in and all alone without her family.

She, this young child, obviously didn't know what was happening to her, trying to figure out who all these strange children were and who were these women with the long black gowns, heads covered in black cowls, looking like scarecrows, and who wanted her to smile as they took a picture! She wasn't happy. She looked terrified, knowing she was only recently snatched away from her whole family. Little Margaret Mary looked annoyed that these people wanted to take her photograph to make it look like all was well at Nazareth House. Margaret was certainly not in the mood for smiling, then or possibly ever again, whilst in that awful building.

I then received a photo of a group of us standing in front of a slide a benefactor had bought for the children, as I mentioned earlier in this book. I was around aged seven in this photo, I believe. Meanwhile, I was still in shock over these recent revelations and couldn't sleep or eat for a while. I was physically sick, wondering what would happen next? After a month or so, we had planned to get a petition together to call for an inquiry into institutional abuse here in Northern Ireland, just as had happened in the South of Ireland and which was still ongoing. We drew up A4 pages and printed them out, ready for when it was right to set out on the road asking people if they would sign the petition. Around this time, I finally dared to start documenting things on my computer. Memories I managed to fearfully recall as that young child who, along with others, had endured the cruelty, the beatings, the theft of personal property, the bullying, torment and torture that had occurred week in and out for many years. On reading what had poured out from my fingertips, I cried uncontrollably, grieving for the child in me. In doing so, my usual cover of protection had broken as I continued to type.

The writing that I had added to on alternate days when I felt a little more able to, was finally sent to the Motherhouse hierarchy in Hammersmith London. In response, this was sent it on to the Nazareth HQ in Dublin, who in return sent it back up north to Nazareth House HQ, in Belfast. No one seemed to want to take responsibility for what was stated in the letter, my letter of complaint. I then sent the letter to the head of the RC Church of Ireland Cardinal Sean Brady, who responded telling me how very well written it was and that he would pray for me and others.

After seeing her speak on the TV, the lady I connected with and I contacted a small newspaper outlet, the South Belfast News, which was the catchment area where the Nazareth-run institutions were based. Whatever I had typed out and printed, I entrusted to one female journalist, who gave it front page news almost weekly, with headlines shaming the religious orders asking for a statement in response and as a right of reply. No response was forthcoming from them once again as they hid behind the walls of canon law protocol, as they always did. There were accurate reports that those who worked for and supported the orders, at that time, had bought many of the midweek newspapers off the shelves in the local shops and on the road near their bases, so no one could read the latest news of what had happened in their buildings. We were told this from shop assistants who worked in the newsagents.

Besides doing the newspaper interview, I had been told by the woman who had been on the TV exposé that another big-time BBC NI producer from the Spotlight programme wanted to do an investigative documentary into the so-called Poor Sisters of Nazareth and to uncover the truth into the abuse of little children under their care. So, when the producer, Darragh McIntyre, called to my house to see me, I was somewhat unaware of what exactly he wanted me to do, such was my bewilderment at what was suddenly taking place...and though I did listen to him as best I could, I was still in disbelief. I assumed the other women would be doing interviews with him, certainly not me...there was no way he could want me to go on tv, could he? I was still in a complete daze from what had recently taken place. Of course, I previously hadn't given my name to the small newspaper outlet, asking the journalist to protect my identity for the moment so that my children and friends would not know where I had been placed as a child.

So how could I ever allow so many people now, to know all about me and my siblings? I didn't realise what I was fully taking on myself. After all this time for me to begin disclosing where I had been in my early years, to reveal my secrets, what would people think? The shame of doing so would kill me. So many emotions almost choked me, practically smothering me into silence, not realising I was in deep shock. I walked around in disbelief, as if in a bad dream.

Before I knew it, and after many weeks of casually chatting with him, Darragh had a small camera team in my house. With my final and full agreement, the camera operators began rolling. They were hidden discreetly in the stair hallway as we both started talking. I saw myself as this baby in the photograph, lined up with others, dressed in ragged, poorly fitted dresses and many with no socks. I mentioned how I just wanted to cuddle the little girl, talking about her in the third person, as it hurt me too much to believe this little child was *me*. I spoke of the many times week in and out of being cruelly scrubbed with deck brushes in cold baths, almost drowned in a strong lethal disinfectant that should only have been used in animal yards. We were dipped like little lambs taken from a filthy flea-ridden sheep pen. Children were forced to run a gauntlet of terror before being thrown out into the cold again, humiliated and dumped like unwanted stray dogs. Locked up in dark cupboards and storerooms as punishments for hours on end into the dark of night without light, beaten with sticks and belts, bunches of keys, and other abuses that were meted upon us.

I sat in my living room talking to Darragh, close to tears. He was a perfect gentleman and not coercive or demanding, allowing my thoughts and memories to come more freely in answer to his gentle questions. In no time at all, the filming was over. I didn't fully realise what I had done. I was still quite numb, refusing to believe what was taking place. Suddenly, in the next few weeks or so, we were informed that the programme was being aired, and the coming extracts of it were being shown on TV well before the due date of its running, which was on its usual Thursday night slot. I was asked by the production team how many signatures I had already collected for the petition and if it was possible, perhaps, that they could film me the next time I was on the streets doing so.

This coverage of my asking for signatures was to fit into the documentary, and I found myself readily agreeing to this request. Within a few days, I walked through the city centre, asking people if they wished to sign it. Not one person refused, with many telling me of their own stories or incidents of abuse they, or family members, had endured also. It seemed like they already somehow knew what had been going on, not only in these institutions but within the community for a very long time, though not many ever dared to speak out about it.

Something was changing amongst the usually compliant and loyal religious people in the neighbourhoods. They would no longer be brainwashed into keeping silent or continue living in fear. They now had a voice and spoke out in support by signing their names, demanding an inquiry into religious and state-run institutional abuses. The woman on the first tv news item all those months ago that I'd contacted, and who lived in England, had been in Belfast a few times but couldn't remain here as she had her own life at home in England. Hence, I found someone to stand with me, many times in the pouring rain, if only to get more signatures put to the petition, which was now growing. I didn't want only a few thousand, I tried to get as many as possible, and they were forthcoming everywhere I walked or stood. I wasn't sure who would be on the up-and-coming spotlight programme with me. I still couldn't understand what I had done and what I was doing now.

So, here I was in the company of a male friend of whom I was grateful for having his company. He who offered to stand with me and, as he had said, had 'nothing better to do'. Amazingly with him doing so and whilst he was standing outdoors with me collecting support for the petition, his mind was entirely distracted from alcohol. He was able to break his habit and get off the drink, becoming completely sober, never to touch alcohol again, as I understand.

One day as I was shopping nearby, I started getting phone calls telling me I was on TV. Short sound bites were being shot up on the screen about what would be shown the following Thursday. My heart almost jumped into my mouth when I also managed to view the excerpts. Watching myself talking about myself, albeit as that little young child Margaret Mary was so surreal and almost dreadfully frightening, with me unconsciously asking myself, 'Was this me on BBC television?'

When the final night came around for the entire programme to be shown, I hurriedly yet nervously ran upstairs to my bedroom to watch it all in secret, not wanting any of my three sons to see or hear it, neither did I want them to see me on TV or to know how I felt, as I spoke out. Away from their watching curious eyes, I sat in tears watching it. I couldn't believe this was me and that what was being shown was of interest to thousands, if not millions, of other people. The programme was entitled "Who is Going to Say Sorry?" This question was directed to the Poor Sisters of Nazareth, the religious order which ran not only the institution I was in but many other children's homes throughout Ireland and the UK. A very high-profile academic professor from Ulster University, Deirdre Heenan, gave a commentary piece on the religious orders and church hierarchy in Ireland, speaking on the taboo and the shame the church felt that was placed upon them. They were now having to look after the children, the waifs and strays of fallen women and those of us who now, according to the nuns, carried the sins of our mothers. This is how we were labelled, even though many children like me had a family and were not orphaned. The nuns called us all orphans, though they had no right to label or stigmatise any child in such a cruel and uncaring manner. These remarks and put-downs damaged us children much more than their beatings, I felt.

The name-calling stayed with children for a lifetime into adulthood and old age, with us believing and seeing ourselves as the lowest of the low, unwanted, stained, sinful and imperfect. The religious felt they were doing us all a favour by accepting us into their convents, scrubbing us clean of sin in lethally strong disinfectant, and praying away the disease of impurity in a deep cleansing ritual.

The second part of the programme went on to raise the stories of other ex-residents, who had spoken out of the violent abuse they went through as children and of how the nuns and their sidekicks beat them mercilessly. Revelations of the many times when sent out on holidays to farms across the North of Ireland where they had been sexually and physically abused, though never believed by the nuns on return to the institutions. They too told also of being put into dark cupboards overnight, refused food as punishment, or force-fed with one's vomit when sick. This was exactly how I remembered it yet more confirmation of how the nuns used us all. Listening to harrowing accounts of how one's hair was scrubbed roughly in boiling water, poured from giant jugs over our bent heads that got pushed into the overflowing tin tubs below our faces. Tales of getting deloused by scraping through our tender scalps with a large, heavy steel nit comb made us bleed and cry in pain and agony, standing in line, shaking in trauma as we knew what was about to take place this every week. It was torturous to endure, but more so, as to now hear it from others, it just brought it back again, almost akin to living through it as it was relayed from former residents.

'Torture' was a word and description used by three High Court Judges later during the campaign years to describe what we as children suffered. I did not know all the people who took part in the programme, though I recalled three of the women who spoke out, as they had been in the same institution as myself. Around that same time I had recently met two men who had been resident in the same institutions as my brothers and as they told me what they went through, I immediately thought again of what they had gone through.

It was shocking and so sad to hear what had happened to them all, and when they spoke, it brought to my mind instances of many other things I'd been put through, stuff that I'd kept hidden for many years. I was like a pressure cooker, simmering with memories, and now, the lid was lifted open. It seemed now was the safest time to release anything I was holding inside, knowing this was not just about me but for many other thousands of abuse victims of state and church, to speak out and to be listened to.

In the past, many voices had been silenced and not believed. Now there was no going back. The floodgates had opened, and many would follow through with us this time. I was determined I was in this for the long haul. Come what may! The documentary was shown, the truth began to seep out and I had finally allowed some people into my otherwise very private, hidden past life. This was only the beginning. My phone didn't stop ringing. So many people called in shock at what had just happened, at what they had just seen and heard on BBC1 TV. Many supported me in speaking out, as it was so well known that the church held much power over its people, with not many before this time daring to speak out about them.

Similar investigations had already begun to unfold in the South of Ireland. Now it seemed, was the right time to probe into church and state institutional abuse in the North of Ireland, just as Carmel Hanna of the Social Democratic and Labour Party (SDLP) Members of the Legislative Assembly (MLA) politicians had forewarned and predicted. Still, many refused to say a word against the church and religious orders. Such was the power still wielded over them, with many of the faithful fearing that they would burn in hell for their sins of speaking out against the churches. This is what so many of the parishioners believed, along with many other of the age-old misleading teachings of Irelands religious doctrines.

The following week, many reporters phoned me looking for interviews. I was guided firstly by political representative, Carmel Hanna, to whom I had given a copy of my letter of complaint, along with her special adviser, Anna McAlister. We spoke of Carmel's recent decision to place a motion into the NI Stormont Assembly calling for the government to be prepared and ready for a deluge of similar complaints as had already happened in the South of Ireland. She had envisaged correctly, as they were the same religious organisations throughout Ireland.

The day the motion was debated by MLAs of every party, we were all present on the balcony, watching and listening closely to how politics worked and how it did not at many stages. After a lengthy debate, the motion was passed, with only one party refusing to agree. Unsurprisingly, the main unionist party said it wasn't 'their' responsibility but that of the Roman Catholic Church itself! This summing up from them would be found categorically untrue and wrong in the future, as the fault and blame lay with the Protestant and Catholic State and Churches!

The Historical Institutional Abuse (HIA) campaign had begun, and the journey to achieve justice for survivors and victims of State and Church child abuse was starting to gain support from politicians after we held various meetings in venues with all party MLAs who finally agreed to help us in our quest. After thousands of signatures had been collected by those showing their support for an inquiry, the petition was taken up to Stormont parliament buildings to be handed to the house speaker. It was the first-ever petition to be brought to its buildings, Carmel Hanna and I were told, with history being made that day, though much more was to be revealed and made along the way.

Conall McDevitt and Anna McAllister had taken over from Carmel, and they sat with us at one meeting after another, calling for an inquiry. However, many politicians needed to learn how this would be done, under what Act and how it would be run, and who would pay for it. One Stormont department seemed to blame the other, saying it was the other's responsibility. This time-wasting debacle went on for quite some time, after communicating whilst the TV cameras were rolling exactly how they would support us! However, what some MLAs said in front of the cameras was much different away from rolling cameras, failing to follow through on what they promised. I was so angry that I continued doing weekly interviews, calling for meetings with MLAs and civil servants - anyone who might listen. It would take a while for them to do so. Soon enough, however, they would cave in!

CHAPTER EIGHT

Although the campaign for an inquiry into care homes and training schools had started, my fellow campaigners and I had only gotten so far. More was needed. I had learned that if the momentum slowed down, the campaign could very quickly be forgotten about by politicians, civil servants and others. We continued to lobby for an inquiry through non-stop media interviews, both on radio and TV talk shows, and so many times, getting excellent coverage on the front page of newspapers nationwide.

In doing so, I got to know many supportive and helpful contacts in almost every media outlet throughout Ireland and further afield who were always keen to keep the story in the news. Around this time, there were many televised reports of allegations of clerical abuse of young men and women by parish priests and religious orders. Also, mismanagement in the churches because of the blatant coverup and denials regarding the investigations into repeated ungodly behaviours that occurred in church parishes and beyond. It appeared that Ireland was going through a thorough shaking, a cleansing out of the church and the dioceses, noticeably with weekly and monthly exposés of sexual abuse and coverup claims. There were allegations of wrongdoings in the religious seminars of young men who were training as seminarians, stating that they had been either groomed or sexually assaulted by priests as they resided in the enclosed private cells well away from the public and prying eyes.

These ongoing reports and calls for inquiries in the South of Ireland ultimately challenged the once romantic, poetic view that Ireland was once poignantly known as the land of saints and scholars.

This shocking and vile news spread worldwide, with many calls coming daily for the immediate resignations of high-profile church figures, bishops and cardinals. The country was in uproar and disbelief that such occurrences had taken place. The once 'unspoken' news began to be widely publicised. The public, or those that chose to believe the emerging truth, were incensed and outraged that those who held to the church's beliefs were now being made a mockery of at the hands of those who towered over them, those who at many times in their weekly sermons condemned them to hell for their minor misdemeanours.

At the corner grocery store, the truth was out, pouring out. A wide range of local and overseas journalists were constantly looking for someone to give interviews. This resulted in hordes of former church-going Catholics to disown the church. Around this time, the Vatican and the Pope himself was asked to intervene and to disown and remove the 'wolves in sheep's clothing' who, like the Vatican, continued to cover up their dastardly deeds by sending the paedophile priests away to foreign countries, to continue their vile practices!

I was again asked to comment on these shameful atrocities within the church. I readily agreed to and commented on these as nothing surprised me at this time, hence my calling also for their resignations with the hope to bring about prosecutions.

It was notable at this time that the BBC producer and investigative journalist, Darragh McIntyre, was the same person who had been pivotal and privy to this inside information and of the many sordid details that had taken place throughout Ireland, especially in the many church dioceses in the South. Darragh was now at the helm of many documentaries and investigations.

Meanwhile, this time of change gave me the belief and momentum to keep fighting for what I and others believed in, not taking no for an answer. We kept badgering those who could help make that change run smoothly and efficiently. I had begun to learn how government officials operated, finding out through trial and error what they really meant when making statements and giving responses to questions asked on our behalf in the Northern Ireland assembly in Stormont parliament buildings. Along with the civil service, they used a type of 'civil service speak,' a coded, insider language, making one believe that they were doing their jobs efficiently.

Because of not hearing back swiftly enough from any minister at Stormont after writing to them, I demanded meetings with them, this firstly at the behest of my MLA contacts and our loyal political activists. If that didn't work, I would again get on to the radio stations and tell listeners we were being ignored by politicians who were not doing their jobs properly. Some ministers, or their Special Advisors (SPAD), were getting fed up with my demands and were not as committed as they had seemed to be at first. We asked so many questions and received very few answers. Finally, we heard that they still needed to figure out what to do or how to organise and set up an inquiry, passing the buck and remit on to education, health sectors etc., with each department putting the onus on each other's shoulders and vice versa.

We continued giving them every reason why it should happen urgently, attending meetings with politicians, some church figures, and civil servants and always having the media on standby after every session. We knew the lack of results from the Government would be yet another unwanted blemish upon them, knowing it would receive headline news, and it always, without fail, did! With the extended almost daily media coverage we were receiving in the North, not to mention what was happening in the South of Ireland, we knew the Government would have to cave in and set a date sooner rather than later.

Throughout the early and subsequent years, many hundreds of abuse victims contacted me just to let me know what had happened to them whilst under the care of various religious orders and state-run institutions and of churches. Hearing of this, week in and out, made me more determined that this Government and church should be held accountable and an inquiry should be set up immediately.

Many people who came forward were elderly and ill, mainly from carrying their secrets for a lifetime, never telling families or friends, this being the first time they had ever told anyone. I made lots of contacts with these women and men. I invited them along to protests and gatherings up the long walk and hill to parliament buildings in Stormont, the front of city hall in Belfast, or wherever we could get noticed and supported by councillors, politicians, and the public. We encouraged each other to speak out, to fight for our right to be listened to and to receive justice by making sure our abusers would be investigated and put on trial. We took to the streets with banners made of white sheets and wrote on them with markers or paint. We didn't care what they looked like. We wanted all to read our message and for us to be seen and heard!

Vowing never to give up until someone finally agreed to our calls for an inquiry, we kept it going. However, along the way, many older adults got disheartened, thinking it would never happen. I didn't blame them, but I had enough fight for them all. I would continue with a few others who would permanently fill the ranks, coming up from the rear when others fell out of line. Too many of our people felt humiliated by the Government, once again re-traumatised, daring to open up into revealing their pasts, some on live TV, radio and in newspapers, only to get nowhere, such was the non-urgent demeanour, stance and uncaring attitudes of those residing in Stormont with their SPADs in tow. All of us were mentally exhausted and in disbelief that those in authority once again would treat its citizens like this. It was almost soul-destroying, but we kept moving forward.

This went on for a few years before the Government decided to bow to pressure only, I believe, because of the relentless media coverage and our persistent calling out for them to do so. We now had our select group of genuine caring MLAs who always stepped up for us, and they, along with ourselves, repeated the demands for an inquiry. I had much earlier been warned that the civil service were not always on the ball, in preparing and getting started or finishing any course of the business venture at Stormont. This was indeed so very true, as we would find out. I needed to learn the government business's ins and outs and daily workings. Still, I believed that those in power who had been paid to be of service to others should act accordingly and do what is right and just for its citizens.

At long last, on hearing the lead politicians (the First and Deputy First Ministers at the time) had decided to announce an inquiry would be held. The media were all over this news. It was released on a snowy winter's evening, and as I walked through the town centre, I heard it through a phone call from a top civil servant of the task force, which was set up and put in place to help prepare the remit and terms of reference of the inquiry.

Media outlets wanted to get a comment on this long-awaited news finally arriving, with them wanting to get an interview immediately for the late-night news bulletins. Once again, I found myself in the TV studios with an MLA, Conall McDevitt, who had supported us from the beginning of the campaign. Things would run very rapidly now that we had reached this agreement. It was not to be, as so much had to be sorted out and put into place. Unfortunately, the fierce lobbying had to begin again to get them to hurry along in getting the inquiry up and running, preparing the terms of reference details, decisions on where it would be held and by whom, and so many other technicalities to be brought forward. Slow could have accurately described the length of time they took to do this. Once again, it was at a snail-pace crawl every inch of the way. As usual and as before, it appeared to us that it was another stalling process, with excuses coming one after another as to why it wasn't up and running much quicker. This caused us much stress and anxiety, as many more victims passed away while waiting for the inquiry. I didn't believe it would take so much energy and fierce, relentless lobbying to get them to do what they had promised.

Finally, we got the word that we had waited on for quite a few long years. The HIA Inquiry was to go ahead and commence soon, after Mike Nesbitt (Ulster Unionist Party) UUP and Alliance Party's Chris Lyttle had spearheaded the way with us along with another few MLAs with repetitive forceful lobbying. Various parts of the HIA Inquiry would unfold with a personal storytelling phase, whereby people could tell professional counsellors about their experiences in care homes or training schools.

The next phase was to be the inquiry itself and for those who wished to give their evidence in an old courthouse that would be used for the proper investigation. The HIA Inquiry was held in Banbridge Co. Down, led by Sir

Anthony Hart, who was to be the Inquiry Chair. The terms of reference decided to cover all denominational churches and state-run institutions in Northern Ireland. These included the notorious Kincora Boys' Home, training schools, borstals, and youth custody centres. We were quite annoyed firstly at it being held in this old courthouse so many miles away from Belfast, as civil servants decided on and agreed that the inquiry would be held in a recently modernised building in the city centre. Former high court Judge Hart decided upon the courthouse, and that is what he got, such was his already renowned dominance and high-profile respect as a no-nonsense high court judge.

The first tranche of witnesses gave their evidence to the inquiry chairman and a panel of two others. It was traumatic for those to do so and to relive and speak out publicly about what they had gone through at the hands of their violent abusers. This same scenario happened daily, with many crying on the witness stand. Many felt they were on trial as our people could not have our own solicitors speak for us, unlike the Christian brothers and the other religious order organisations.

The inquiry solicitors themselves took down our statements. In hindsight, we should have stood our ground and demanded we had our solicitors prepare them for us, knowing we had already built a relationship with them. As the months went by, it grew much more challenging for us to be present there, as the religious orders sat in the same seating area as ourselves and took their tea breaks at the tiny hot water urns along with us in the same queue. This was not wanted nor needed by us, bringing back horrid memories - just being in the same place as them and it being a very small compact area.

They, of course, gave their evidence, always denying that these atrocities happened, their highly paid lawyers standing before them, protecting them, attempting to diminish the truth by declaring they were lies. Though on many good days for us, evidence appeared to show how the institutions would treat the children like slaves, who were forced to do all the work in the buildings, scrubbing on their knees, laying in cold dark rooms overnight as a punishment, brutalised by straps, hawthorn sticks and bunches of heavy keys. Hair hacked off with shears in front of others, mocked in humiliation as a warning to behave, or more so just because the nuns had grown tired of their so-called alleged vocation and appeared to visibly hate their job, who then took it out on innocent children. Not to mention the sexual abuse carried out by predators, priests, and so many others who took vile advantage of children in their care.

All was now finally being revealed, the worst unimaginable sexual abuse and assaults being carried out by Christian brothers in Rubane House in Co Down and by loyalist paedophiles who worked in Kincora House another notorious institution for young teenage boys in East Belfast. The inquiry lawyers read evidence of the Christian brothers sending the children out to work on farms in the cold, unfed and with ragged clothes, fingers bleeding as they picked potatoes and vegetables in the harsh winters, and throughout all seasons, working as manual labourers with heavy-duty farm appliances and throwing them into an old cold, freezing swimming pool. Even though they could not swim, they were stripped in the school every morning making them bend over desks in front of others, whilst beating them with a thick heavy strap fitted with coins and pieces of lead, making them bleed. And why? Potentially for their sexual gratification, perhaps? It was known and testified that the religious orders didn't want government bodies knowing what was going on inside their buildings, instead wanting sole power and overall decisions made by themselves with no outside forces intervening. In so doing, they refused to receive any funding or benefits from the Government to help with our care and upbringing, so they wouldn't have to comply with allowing inspections and to have receipts and accountability for what was paid for and used in the welfare of children under their care!

The testimonies of the former children, now adults, were harrowing. Heart-breaking stories were given by many older adults who had been shipped out on boats illegally as very young children, infamously known now as child migrants. These children were selected and examined thoroughly, firstly making sure they were of 'good stock'...before being sent like cattle on a ship to the other side of the world to Australia to join up with yet other religious order-run institutions, whereby the children could be used for unpaid manual labour. The horrors that met them when they arrived and what they lived

132

through over the years spent there away from their own country were read out as more and more evidence unfolded from the lawyers and the association for child migrants and former individual migrants themselves.

The wide-ranging evidence disclosed in the old courthouse in Banbridge Co. Down, where the Hart Inquiry into Historical Institutional Abuse was held, covered a sizeable cross-community section of victims and survivors. All had a story to tell. At long last, many had finally been listened to after their cries for help in the past had been dismissed, frowned upon and never believed. After the inquiry hearings ended, the Chair, Sir Anthony Hart and his panel studied what remained of the colossal bundles of evidence. Having previously compiled proof of abuse from the modules already covered up to closing, he ended things. We were told they would decide on the findings as soon as possible. With the judge realising the length of time victims had waited and who had already endured a lifetime of suffering, the day arrived when a hotel on the outskirts of Belfast was to be used for the inquiry findings. All media across the world were notified and on standby. A few of us stayed overnight at the hotel to be notified of the findings before the news got out to the public. Modules of every institution covered at the inquiry were printed into ten volumes.

We received sight of these a few hours beforehand, and many had gathered at the hotel to hear Sir Anthony's decision. We sat before him in tears of joy, relief and somewhat sadness. So many mixed emotions had overcome us. He stated loudly from the podium that physical, sexual abuse and neglect had been systemic in the majority of the church and state-run institutions and, particularly he called out, in Nazareth House and Lodge and Rubane House Kircubbin run by the De La Salle Orders and Kincora boys home. The media were waiting everywhere and many had asked for pre-recorded interviews which I always agreed to. I wanted the world to know every detail of what was occurring over the long years of the campaign. They were a big part of this journey with me. We all thanked the panel for coming to this decision and hoped that upon releasing the complete recommendations, they would be delivered and acted on as soon as possible. This was a day we had waited on for a lifetime for someone in authority to tell us...we were right. We believed that our abusers were in the wrong and that they needed to be punished, not us!

However, a few days later, Stormont fell because of the ongoing squabbling that was a regular occurrence between the two main leading political parties. No government business could occur or be signed off by Ministers, as there was no government. Sinn Fein had walked out because of the RHI Cash for Ash scandal and certain MLAs reneging on their promises. The inquiry recommendations, including a redress board for compensation and a services package, could not be delivered to survivors and victims of institutional abuse! We didn't dare to think this collapse of Government would be long and drawn out. It couldn't happen to us again, could it? Not after the long struggle of finally getting to this pivotal point and an end to the inquiry, with the Hart Inquiry findings finding favour with us in believing our stories, our complaints. Sir Anthony Hart stated that his and the inquiry panel's recommendations were to include a monetary payment which he said should be swiftly paid out to older people and the infirm whilst waiting on the setting up of a scheme to deliver on compensation pay-outs.

After long months of stalemate, with either side politically not giving an inch and no sign of Stormont getting back up and running again soon, we decided to lobby again and protest wherever we could be noticed and heard. We also took a judicial review to the courts stating that, indeed, the civil servants who were now in charge could deliver an Ex Gratis payment as in the legislation of the Hart Findings, overseen by the acting top head of the civil service. The lawyers for the Executive Office denied this was the case, saying they did not have the power to do so and that only ministers in Government could act on signing off and delivering a payment scheme.

On hearing these constant refusals to deliver, we decided to bring it to the Crown Courts to allow them to decide for us all. However, a stalemate took place after many months, with the judge and barristers making legal points of order for either side. A single sitting judge, who assumed the Government would be up and running very soon, (having been told this by the opposition barristers), left him not wanting to act on our case, stating he believed Stormont Ministers would be in place very soon.

We were distraught by his decision and went further by taking our case to the high courts of appeal. This case was being heard and put back constantly over many months, running into a year. We met with the NI Home Office and Secretaries of State, of which many came and went. Such was the state of politics not only here in Northern Ireland but now also there were chaotic scenes at Westminster, with their latest Prime minister Boris Johnson.

He had threatened and was about to prorogue all business at parliament buildings in the House of Commons, just as we had met with the latest Tory Secretary of State (SoS), Julian Smith. We began to trust him, unlike his predecessors...but now this was about to happen! On the days leading up to our final court of appeal hearing to question and to confront the NI Executive office that they could deliver on the Hart Inquiry findings, which they denied. We had been fiercely lobbying all MPs and the House of Lords members, all former MLAs and finally, church leaders to help sway favour on our behalf. I wrote to the Catholic church leaders here in NI, pleading with them to intervene and appeal to the Westminster business manager Jacob Rees Moggs, a staunch Roman Catholic, to allow our business to go through.

Father Tim Bartlett, a more modern and much younger Catholic priest compared to the elderly old school type, was a decent and kindly friend to myself and my colleague Kate over the years of the campaign trail. He responded to my requests and agreed to write a letter for me, telling me I could use it to give to Westminster MP Jacob Rees Moggs and PM Boris Johnston. Fr. Tim emailed me the letter that same day in response to my pleading that we needed it urgently and imminently, seeing that all government business in Westminster was closing before our eyes. I immediately gave the letter to SoS Julian Smith and his team in the NI office who were all delighted at getting this priceless piece of the jigsaw, which, hopefully, we all dared to believe could be the vital piece that got us over the line.

Meanwhile, the next day was 'decision time' at the High Court of Appeal in Belfast. As usual, a long-awaited decision to our JR80 (Judicial Review) case was to be given throughout this relentless fight for justice. We couldn't sleep as we waited to find out if the battle, as it were, would go our way or for the NI government. We arrived at the courthouse and found our usual media contacts lined up as they had always faithfully done. They supported us throughout our continuous battle rounds over the many years of our campaign and combat.

Our motley crew walked through the steel gates and heavy security doors once more in pursuit of justice...a justice we had been given a few years back and one that had been as quickly snatched away from us. We hoped and prayed that this day would be ours and that what we had achieved and the decisions that the HIA Inquiry chairman had made, would be returned to us by taking this court case.

The three judges, in their summing up, finally gave their decisions. All three agreed that the Executive Office could introduce and deliver an Ex-Gratis Payment as part of the compensation scheme resulting from the HIA Inquiry findings. On finishing their opinions and agreed decisions, the three judges said that 'what we had already gone through was torture and now to have to go through yet more uncertainty after getting so far was cruel and uncalled for'. In summing up, the judges stated that we had suffered enough in life and coming through the collapse of Stormont and the government was yet another abuse upon our already feeble state of mind. Now, with no ministers in charge to sign off on the inquiry findings, its collapse meant innocent victims were left living in a state of limbo. Many were left uncertain with regard to what was going to happen to them next, whether they would still be alive to receive compensation, especially as so many had already passed on whilst waiting.

They had agreed that this court case JR80 should not have had to happen, saying that if the Executive Office had done their jobs efficiently and correctly and if they had acquired the professional legal advice needed, we wouldn't have had to go through yet another traumatic struggle in our lives. The media were lined up and waited on us outside the High Court as we walked out triumphantly, with our fists in the air, rejoicing in this decision and our victory against the mighty Government and its officials. I spoke up loudly in front of the microphones, letting the whole of the Stormont

Government know what we thought of them for repeatedly putting us through this trauma, treating us with disdain as if we were the lowest of the low, thinking we wouldn't question their authority. They got that wrong, along with so many other issues. We didn't give up, we refused to back down, and once again, we were proven to be in the right, and they were proven to be in the wrong, by three highly esteemed high court judges. Oh, what a day!

I reminded them in speaking boldly and directly into the TV cameras that they now needed to get back to work and do as the three judges had just said they had the power to do, to set up the compensation scheme in preparation for what we had fought for and were now flying to London directly to demand its legislation be fast tracked through Westminster. Straight after the court decision, a taxi was waiting to bring me and a colleague to the airport, flying over to meet with the NI Secretary of State and his staff belonging to the NI Office.

After we landed in London, we immediately met with various contacts supporting us, those from the House of Lords and some MPs who had agreed to meet with me and Anna McAllister. Anna was very much politically aware and educated. Such was her profession.

At the House of Commons, its last day of business drew near, and we knew there wouldn't be much sleep yet again as we awaited the following day. We had hoped that by meeting up with even more influential people who knew the ins and outs of Government, they would lend their support by putting more pressure upon the leaders of the day. The next day after another series of meetings and with some uncertainty as to what would happen, we, along with our solicitor friend and colleague, Claire McKeegan, met up with other long-time friends from the past and proceeded to walk together through security and into the House of Commons.

Claire, Anna and I waited around, in between meetings, until we got the nod that it was going ahead and that our legislation would miraculously be put through somehow. I just knew it would have to be passed. I couldn't have taken no for an answer after getting so close. I had already warned them all jokingly and half-heartedly that if it didn't go through, 'Guy Fawkes Day' would occur again, and it certainly would not fail this time.

We all sat in the chamber in the gallery as we listened to one MP after another give their support for our case. Then it was Julian Smith, our NI SoS, turn to speak. By the time he got to read out Fr. Tim Bartlett's letter, Julian's voice had broken as he began reading. He teared up as he read the heartfelt words Fr. Tim had written, mainly when he came to the lines which said... "I appeal to you, Prime Minister and Business Manager, please don't let these people down again. We had already failed them as children when they asked to be cherished and cared for. We, on many occasions, failed them. Instead of nurturing and showing them love and compassion, we let them down, leaving them as defenceless young children to suffer dreadfully and shamefully in our institutions. Please don't allow them to go through this rejection yet again".

On receiving that letter, both JR Moggs and PM Boris Johnson allowed only our business case to go through that day, as all other businesses throughout the UK stopped and failed to proceed indefinitely.

Immediately after that, Westminster closed for business. We had watched as it was fast-tracked and agreed on in both houses, the House of Lords and the House of Commons and now finally, with the Queen's permission, signed off.

What a fight, what a struggle, but it was a victorious battle and one fight without me having to get into a fisticuffs wrestling match or getting arrested by the police or being placed in jail for disorderly behaviour! I knew now that I had turned a very long, endless corner, that I could fight and win these days differently without turning to petty juvenile violence...Thank God for that.

Next, it was to oversee the setting up of the Redress Board and Scheme, the specific Services for Survivors and Victims of Institutional Abuse. So many are still coming forward, mainly because of the massive publicity we have acquired over the years. The fight was still not over, and we had to, unbelievably, once again, lobby hard with the Stormont Government and its civil servants to get this in place. Our battle continued.

CHAPTER NINE

Setting up the redress scheme for abuse victims brought about upsets and problems for many of us. With the very well-publicised campaign and the considerable achievement of having an inquiry, the positive findings and finally, the setting up of the Redress Board, all wasn't ready to settle down just yet. The Scheme itself wasn't up and running as swiftly as we would have hoped it would be. We had to wait for the various panels as part of the board to be in place. Board members had to be fully trained and legally permitted to distribute compensation awards to those abused throughout several institutions and training schools.

These statutes and laws had all been written into and came under the terms of reference, as stated in the HIA (Historical Institutional Abuse Inquiry) legislation that was only recently put into law and fast-tracked through Westminster. The Institutions that had been investigated had already been given fair warning that they would all have to contribute to the compensation pot, depending on the outcome of the Inquiry and the many involved in abusing those children in its care. The pay-outs determined on what form of abuse one had endured or suffered while residing in the care of state and church-run institutions across Northern Ireland.

By the time this Scheme was up and running, all life had been practically drained out of all-too-many elderly and infirm people. It was simply too much for them. The hope and the trust that we had finally dared to put into authority figures, the daring to believe that this government would now, at long last look after them with compassion, was dashed again and again, leaving people broken-hearted. The hope that society wouldn't and couldn't let us down again, believing that those in charge would take this time to do what was humane and just - this too fell through, leaving us in a state of hopelessness.

Even after long years of ill health and living with unwanted memories of our childhood abuse and lack of care whilst children, this present situation turned into one long, never-ending nightmare with no one professionally dedicated to counselling those in need nor to helping take the pressure of what one was carrying. Once again, we were left to try to look after each other. I believe people passed away with a broken heart, mentally and emotionally shattered, because they had opened up and told of their once hidden secrets, thinking that doing so would bring them some peace, respite and some form of closure. This vision or dream of peace lasted only briefly, mainly because it took time to set up and deliver the redress scheme and the vital services they desperately needed. There was so much bureaucracy, red tape and excessive adherence to official doctrines and formalities, making it complicated for victims to understand. It wasn't easy or plain sailing for so many of those taking part in applying for compensation. This setup was another obstacle to overcome, another battle and more confusion.

This new and massive piece of legislation, recently drawn up by civil servants and their lawyers, was now set into law and ready to be interpreted or misinterpreted depending on its deliverance and outlook, even by those with a professional eagle eye. More officialdom was most certainly what we didn't need nor want at this time after having to go through years of it already. Already tired and battle-weary from years of having to fight our way through government rules and regulations, we found it exhausting to figure out the complexities of how to apply, with our solicitors and various legal teams having to learn themselves how to go about processing the ins and outs of the Scheme.

By the time the compensation awards finally started to be paid out, many people had just drifted off to their corner of the world, so relieved in not having to wait any longer. They just about stayed alive to believe that this day would finally arrive. So many were disappointed in the pay-outs, and I can understand why in many cases. However, it did seem to depend on what institution one was in and the level of abuse found by the inquiry panel to have occurred in either of these individual care homes or training schools. It was found that 'systemic abuse' did not occur in all of them. My belief, and that of the majority, was that the top award was a pittance and an absolute insult to victims after what some of the ex-residents had gone through in the care system. Their lives had been completely ruined, becoming practically lifeless because of what they had endured whilst there, not to mention what they had gone through on release.

A huge number of men and women could just not survive or cope in society on the outside, with many having become so institutionalised. However, these were the findings and outcomes of Sir Anthony Hart, the former High Court Judge and the Chair of the HIA Inquiry, and realising it would have taken so much time and perhaps years to attempt changing the legislation regarding the amount of compensation that was to be awarded, we agreed not to prolong the waiting of the most vulnerable and to not legally challenge the decision. None of us had the time or energy to do so anymore. The final stages of the findings that had to be acted on were the HIA Apology and the Memorial. These would once again have to be lobbied for in the future. In the meantime, I knew it was more important to get through the hiccups of the applications and settlements in redress, in which so many had continued contacting me daily to assist or speak out on their behalf.

This once again had taken its toll on me, with friends telling me constantly that I needed to stand aside and rest myself. I could feel my body and mind so heavily overloaded with fifteen years of campaigning that I was mentally and emotionally destroying myself; unable to manage a good night's sleep because of waking up with nightmares, but also with the worries and stresses of feeling the need to help others. I soon, along with others, began noticing I was slurring my words and couldn't speak clearly at times. My head felt like it was exploding with so many unanswered questions.

I couldn't cope with taking any more phone calls or reading messages on social media, so I finally agreed to stop doing so. I was going through a breakdown, and under the orders of my doctor and a few close friends, the deleting of Facebook and my other social media accounts began. A close friend offered to do this for me with my full permission and agreement. Having been contacted by many looking for help and guidance over the years, I just had to stop reading messages, as they kept me up late into the night. The non-stop calls and texts from people from all areas and regions across Ireland and the UK and abroad were relentless.

My heart went out to those going through the torment of not being heard or dealt with properly, which deeply affected me. Everything I did was voluntary as I felt I had to continue helping as it was myself who they contacted after seeing me out front on TV and radio speaking up for everyone and anyone who had gone through the care system. Therefore, they all probably assumed that I was in a fully paid position and I was the 'go-to' person. I couldn't refuse to help or assist anyone. But now, with my own mental health noticeably on a downward spiral, with an inner feeling that I was fragmenting, that I was falling apart at the seams. The wrong belief that I had to be in action mode constantly to intervene and help them all was beginning to leave me. I just couldn't cope or continue to be on call day and night anymore.

The HIA Services were still not up and running fully or adequately. Even in my time of supposed resting from the many years of campaigning, many victims like me suffered severely from mental health issues, PTSD, stress-pain and the need to talk to professionals with specific training in institutional abuse and its traumatic side effects and triggers.

Several months after some rest, I began to raise this urgent matter with supportive MLAs in Stormont parliament buildings and with top civil servants who sat in meetings with us but made no promises to release the funding that had already been put by for this purpose. Nor did they give any understanding that they soon would.

So once again, I began to lobby hard, turning to Twitter storms, emails and whatever else I could do to hopefully embarrass and shame the NI Executive into releasing the funds belonging to HIA victims for their welfare and support. After endless emails with warnings that my solicitor and long-time colleague, Claire McKeegan from Phoenix Law Human Rights firm and I stated we would take the NI Executive back to the High Court once again and beg to leave to challenge their indecision to release the funds to set up our specific Victims and Survivors Services, they caved in and released the monies allowing and enabling the setting up of a more highly credited organisation. This would give HIA victims more professional support services and a care package which was a little more suitable to their needs. This now helped somewhat in those people in need of advice and support could directly contact the Victims and Survivors Services and finally take the burden from me and those of us that had looked after so many throughout the many years of the long campaign for justice, redress and the long-awaited support services.

Thinking of the so many high-profile cases who seriously needed professional support much sooner than at this late stage, one wonders just why our government didn't or wouldn't afford the best to those who needed specific help instead of setting up inadequate facilities that were unsuitable for the needs of abuse victims. We tried our best to do what professionals should have done but didn't. So many were now at a stage ready to be able to pour out what they had kept a secret for many decades. Grown men and women now wanted to tell their stories of the horrific abuse in childhood they had undergone. For many, it was the first time they did so and they were massively overwhelmed with relief to have been allowed to begin revealing that they, too, had been preyed upon by those in charge of them. Pitiful vulnerable people, who now had decided to tell of these heinous assaults, seriously needed urgent professional assistance and support. We felt that we had been left alone to be counsellors, advocates, and, at times, organisers of victims' funerals, always having to be on standby for people, with many phoning to say they were about to take their own lives.

These situations arose many times in the middle of the campaign, even finding out that those close to us had been abused whilst in care, also.

We never dared to think or wanted to believe it would be our family members and friends who would need help. Kate Walmsley, my friend and colleague of our SAVIA Support and Lobby Group, often jumped into action to be at the beck and call of those who didn't seem to have anyone else to talk to or someone to understand them, for sure, we did understand them. We would be able to empathise with them.

Kate had always been by my side. I met her just before I was to attend a pre-arranged meeting with Church leaders in Derry. Her health team had contacted me by phone asking if I could call to visit her saying she needed to speak to me concerning what she had just heard me talking about on her local television. I got chatting to her that same day. My immediate thoughts on meeting her were that her slim shoulders gave the appearance of her carrying a weight that had been so heavy for her for many years. She wanted a lot lifted from her fragile, frail frame.

As Kate began unloading what she had carried alone for many decades, she collapsed in tears, more so in relief than in despair, more so that at last she could tell someone she trusted how she had been manhandled by priests, by nuns and by the system who let her down and who she felt had hated her whilst in a convent run by the Nazareth Nuns in Derry.

This religious order of nuns was the same order who ran the convent in Belfast in which myself and my siblings had been placed, so now, as I listened to the story of her life under their care, it, too, brought me emotionally back to where I had once been. What she told me about was horrifyingly cruel and shocking. Kate spoke of the brutality, beatings, bullying, and starvation meted out to her whilst there. She recounted how she had vomited up her sins after being told she was a sinner so often she felt if she made herself sick, the blackness of her sins would be removed from inside of her. On being ill at times in the dining room, she was forced to feed on her own vomit like so many of us in the Belfast convent.

Much worse was to come from her as she informed me of visitations of two individual priests who she said, at different stages on weekends, had sexually abused her. One, she went on to claim, had conveniently called her in at confession times on Saturdays and who had continued abusing her in the holy sacristy of the small chapel inside the convent. These claims were substantively believed during various proceedings.

On finding out and listening to this horror story of what Kate had endured along with lots of other victims, I somehow, at the back of my mind, knew something similar was what had possibly happened to my brother Kevin. What I feared the most, I was soon to find out did, in fact, happen to him. Hearing about these first-hand accounts and this in the middle of me still trying to campaign for an inquiry, made me even more determined to continue fighting for justice, accountability and recognition that the truth must be told, especially when the victims are related to you, and those in question have become close friends.

Around the same time as I met Kate, who was to accompany me on the last nine years of the campaign, I began to find out, in-between times, what had happened to Kevin my brother and what he had to endure at the hands of those supposedly in charge of him. Kevin had been placed into Nazareth Lodge for boys, aged four, along with our other brother, aged five and myself, aged three; and our sister, aged seven, into Nazareth House for girls. Kevin was released from Nazareth Lodge at age eleven for a few years but then admitted to the notorious Rubane House in Kircubbin run by the infamous De La Salle Christian Brothers.

Kevin was placed there from the age of thirteen to aged sixteen, and when released he managed to get various jobs and kept himself busy, always wanting to earn money. Kevin, I recall then, in that short spell of him being out of institutional care, was always on the go, even somehow able to buy a second-hand Honda 50 motorbike and the purchase of an old beaten-up car. Such was his manner and attitude of not taking no for an answer.

Kevin was a real adventurer travelling by boat to England to visit our relatives and worked there also. He wasn't too shy in asking for a job and was soon well known for his broad smile and calm demeanour, gentleness, kindness and friendly manner, always eager to help anyone who may have needed a helping hand. He had friends in the area where he had stayed and with whom he had previously attended a special school. As the youngest in the family, I don't remember much of his whereabouts, as from the age of sixteen onwards, I too, had mainly been staying elsewhere whenever I could.

For many years, I wasn't fully aware of where Kevin had suddenly disappeared, where exactly he was, and why. I eventually found out, many years later that Kevin had been placed by court order into another notorious institution, Muckamore Abbey Hospital. A magistrate's court had placed him there after an incident over an old bicycle. Kevin was placed there at seventeen, remaining locked up for seventeen years before being moved to another nursing home for another thirty-four years. Kevin is now aged sixty-six. Upon visiting him at the beginning of the campaign, he told me of his beatings in the classrooms and dormitories and around the yards and shower rooms. The heavy-handed assaults, after certain Christian Brothers ordered individual children to strip off, were followed by them being battered with leather straps fitted deliberately and effectively so with coins and pieces of heavy metal lead, no doubt to ensure a more promising effect. The utter cruel and barbaric practice was a well-devised plan of action. I believe it was a thrill-seeking twisted act of sexual gratification and dominance just to get kicks from hearing young children scream and cry, begging for the 'Christian Brothers' to stop their ungodly assaults upon them.

Kevin had told me of these times though I tried so hard not to listen. I didn't want to know or to hear that anything had happened to him. I could hardly bear the pain of listening to what he had gone through. It was quite a while into the campaign that Kevin, on saying he had seen me on television, began to speak more broadly and specifically of other sinister and more severe events that he had endured. He told me that he was often made to play games and that after the games, which he described as 'love games'...he was given sweets, naming the kind of sweets he was given in return for his game playing.

I was shocked and horrified that this would happen to him as he was so vulnerable, young, and innocent. While it began to sink in after my initial disbelief, I was more determined than ever to find out who did this to him and to get these perpetrators brought to court. Kevin spoke more freely as the weeks passed, telling me of Christian Brothers who raped and sexually assaulted him. He could name them along with a priest who had taken him into his bedroom near the farmyard in Rubane house Kircubbin. What was remarkable was his memory. He is still stuck somewhat in the past, yet he remembered the names of most all the people who ran the institution, able to pinpoint areas and instances where the abuses had taken place and by whom. Until now, Kevin had kept all these assaults secret, never to my knowledge, publicly speaking of them.

The damage this had done to him had affected him greatly. Carrying these secrets and the inherent shame and confusion accompanying this is too much for anyone. He, too, just like Kate, had spoken quite fondly of a few people who were genuinely kind to him, recalling times and events that he had enjoyed whilst resident in Rubane House. He mentioned how he was in a band, played a musical instrument, also having been in the boy scouts, working on the farm, milking cows and potato picking in farmers' fields.

On asking further who had assaulted him throughout periods in care, Kevin spoke of how it started as a young boy in Nazareth Lodge with the sexual assaults by older boys in the dormitories. How they, too, played games with him, which was the start of a cycle of sexual abuse by predators who stole my brother's innocence.

We were told the names of these abusers throughout the campaign who ruined the lives of so many young, innocent children. These assaults confused him about right and wrong for the duration of his stay in the care system after being left at the Nazareth Institution so young.

I raised these incidents with the police and kept at them to investigate these allegations with a named priest, though I found out he was now dead as were many of the Christian Brothers who had assaulted him. Some were now too ill to be prosecuted. This outcome was the same for many abuse victims who did not receive full justice. The same excuses were being made throughout Ireland. Yet, many perpetrators were seen out on the golf courses or holidaying in foreign resorts living life to the full whilst supposedly gravely ill with mental health issues or on their deathbeds. The only way open for us was the formal HIA Inquiry and The Redress Board, as the police and the PPS said the cases were too historical and didn't take them to the courts.

And now, to have finally found out and learned of what had occurred to Kevin whilst in Muckamore Abbey Hospital gave me yet more concern for his mental health and well-being, having previously noticed how drastically changed he had become from his normally outgoing, friendly demeanour. The noticeably lively person he used to be, always wanting to live life, to travel and go anywhere and to communicate with others constantly - these traits were no more. He was no longer the brother I had known; he had completely changed from who he was as an individual before being placed into Muckamore. While I had visited him back then, the Kevin I now saw was a very different person, almost a stranger in many ways. He now had become silent, cagey, mistrusting and hesitant in speaking or not wanting to enter into a conversation. Life seemed to have been drained from him. He began smoking non-stop, something I hadn't known of him doing before in earlier life, even after getting out from Rubane House.

Finally, Kevin was transferred to a much more suitable residence, a nursing home in Co Antrim. I visited him more often while he was here and took him to my caravan in Ballycastle. On visiting Kevin and taking him out for weekends, it was as if I was beginning a relationship with a stranger like we hadn't known each other. I noticed Kevin seemed to be in a kind of trance, avoiding eye contact, seemingly staring into nothingness. He was always noticeably tired and distracted. When not in a direct gaze, he was suspiciously looking around him, always curious about where I was driving him, asking who would be there. I didn't know then that the medication he was taking at that time was the reason for these noticeable changes in his whole being, him wanting to go to sleep or go back to his nursing home.

My view, and I am aware I am no medic, is that he was given medication to subdue and silence him. This medication apparently started when he was placed into Muckamore Abbey Hospital whereby, in my thinking, they conveniently and erroneously diagnosed him as having 'schizophrenia' This is where we all noticed a complete change in his behaviour, attitude, and demeanour. The authorities at that time did not even try to get him into some outside living, overseen and run by trained staff and social workers to provide him with a life worth living back into the community.

I believe that Kevin was never what they decided to label him with. Instead, I think they chose to so wrongly and inhumanely place him in a Mental Hospital, misdiagnose him as a schizophrenic, and give him so much medication.

Kate was also very appreciative and so grateful for the genuine care and kindness she received in another institution she had been moved to after what had happened to her in Derry at the hands of nuns, priests, and her elders. She told me with a smile how this training school run by another order of nuns in another county had been a Godsend for her. She spoke warmly of one of the nuns, who, to her, were angels compared to a few of the nuns in the Derry convent.

I took Kate to Co. Armagh to visit a particular nun who had looked after her, thanking her for what she had done for Kate in protecting her, guiding her and teaching her with love and a caring, genuine heart instead of being overlooked and not listened to, as was the case in the former care home she had been in. Kate told me of how this favourite nun showed her how to dress, cook and sew, amongst preparing her for many other ways of life on the outside. This kindness from a nun completely contrasted what she had undergone and received from the Order in Derry.

We had both recognised and agreed that not all nuns and priests were abusers, which we wanted to get clarified at every opportunity, so much so that this group of nuns were so grateful and delighted that we did give them their place.

Kevin and Kate's abusers were never taken to court. They were deemed too ill, with dementia or other forms of mental health, too old, or that in the majority of our cases, not enough evidence was available...It wasn't all about compensation, services, a memorial, or an apology...we wanted them all named and shamed in public. We had to do this ourselves by continuously having a media campaign and fighting to have them exposed. If we hadn't done it, we would still be waiting for the government to do so.

The shame needs to be put upon the government of this day and those in the years gone by for not moving quickly enough to help and refusing to listen to the cries of so many vulnerable children who cried out for so many years, only to be unheard. And yet, sadly, some adults are still crying out for help, love, care and understanding, with so many unanswered questions, as to why all this could have happened at all.

Many statutory bodies should face the blame for the breakdown of family relationships, the lack of natural justice for victims, the non-urgency of police to arrest and place charges on the abusers, magistrate courts with too much power in the signing away of ones to mental hospitals with no full adequate evidence for doing so. Kevin has now begun to speak to me, Kate, and my elder sister, about what he endured whilst in the Mental Health institution after being placed there by a court magistrate.

When I asked about his time at Muckamore he grimaced with pain and anxiety, refusing to talk about it. Recently, he has been a little more open about his time spent in isolation, in the lockups, on ECT treatment (Electroconvulsive Therapy) and other inhumane treatments.

Who was responsible for Kevin, whilst he was in Muckamore Hospital setting, in allowing him to walk into Antrim town centre, away from the Hospital care system, where he was knocked down by military personnel soldiers on a motorbike, causing him to sustain a broken pelvis and severe damage to his leg? Kevin has been left with a limp and a lopsided tilt in the hip area, creating an imbalance and staggered gait as he walks. Kevin was hospitalised for many months after this severe accident.

Meanwhile, yet another high-profile Inquiry has been set up with vulnerable patients' evidence being presently heard by a High Court Judge from family members and hearing from those responsible for patients who had been placed into the care of the Muckamore Abbey Hospital. I shall be representing my brother, Kevin, raising many concerns to this Inquiry into what they have done to him behind those closed doors and why they medicated him as they did.

Meanwhile, the HIA Inquiry was coming to its final stage, with an apology from the religious orders and the state on behalf of those who ran these institutions. This apology would bring the HIA process to an end. This was the next step to get government officials to honour not only the final pieces of the Inquiry's findings but more to end yet another chapter of this ongoing fifteen-year campaign. The apology process was about to commence, with the beginning of the end of this long journey and battle for recognition, acknowledgement and justice.

CHAPTER TEN

I knew it was vital to, first and foremost, see the present HIA Inquiry findings acted upon, delivered and to see this process end before I could fully concentrate and act as Kevin's spokesperson. I wanted to represent him at yet another high-profile abuse inquiry. This separate Inquiry had just been recently set up to enquire into and investigate and determine just how this large hospital unit had allowed many of the patients to be so severely abused and neglected. Many of its patients are suffering from various illnesses and had been mistreated, bereft of proper due care and attention.

Unfortunately, because of the harrowing details that had been exposed throughout the HIA campaign, I just knew how probable and true these recent allegations of abuse upon these patients were. I was now far more open to the fact that my brother had also suffered, even though I tried to believe that he hadn't.

With a lot of first-hand knowledge and with evidence of how vulnerable people had been systematically abused by their so-called carers and those in charge of running these hospitals and care homes, I needed to find out firstly, how and why, my dear brother had so wrongly been placed into yet another state-run institution as a young seventeen-years-old. This had come after only two years of freedom from his last institutionalised setting. It seemed that my campaigning and speaking out for the voiceless was not ending-not just yet.

The end of the HIA campaign was nearing, and planning was now taking place for the Public Apology stage of the inquiry findings. This would come from the leaders of the churches and the state who had responsibility for these Institutions those specifically who had been found compliant for their lack of care, leading to systemic abuse and neglect. This stage took a great deal of pressurising and persuading to impress upon government officials the need to get it up and running as quickly as possible. We already knew how notoriously slow officials were to initiate any type of business acumen in government circles, and these final stages of the inquiry findings were not any different. So, once again, I had to be constant and consistent in non-stop emailing, writing letters, arranging meetings with yet more fierce lobbying of civil servants and politicians and, of course recognising the utmost importance and necessity of having the media on board to broadcast any lack of interest or inefficiency coming from Stormont's public office.

When at last the announcement was made that the apology would take place and a date was set by government ministers, we were delighted. To get this news, at last, was heart-warming and gave many of us campaigners a well-needed lift. It was just what many victims and survivors had wanted to hear, knowing we would now be able to inform friends, family, and those around Ireland, the UK and abroad that it was finally taking place.

A few months went by, and the planned date was imminent when suddenly we received the shocking news that, once again, one of the Stormont lead parties had walked out of government, leaving our apology derailed. The apology was to have been made by the two main party leaders, and now with one party leader jumping ship as it were, we were left adrift, anchorless and left looking for yet another lifeline to rescue us and to somehow get the parties and the process back on board. Conversations and many meetings with discussions around alternatives took place. This was to be the case unless the one party who had walked out of government decided to come back into government.

This was certainly not what I nor many others wanted, as we could not take a gamble on them ever getting back together. At long last and an answer to our prayers, another miracle occurred when we all finally came to an agreement with government officials and the departmental Ministers. The apology should go ahead and be made on the date that had recently been given, and those politicians who 'were in place' should deliver it on behalf of the state, even if one of the two main leaders were not available. An alternate arrangement was made that suited us all.

In the weeks leading up to the apology, many pre-recorded interviews were asked for in preparation for the big day. Even the night before, I was still talking to journalists, such was the huge interest. Lots of arrangements and plans had been put in place, invitations sent out with a fixed allowance of a smaller number of guests and group members allowed to be present because of Covid-19. Thankfully, we suddenly got word that Covid restrictions were now about to be further relaxed on the day before the apology, which allowed for more extra seating arrangements. The preparations had been done; all was seemingly in order. We had got sight of the speeches beforehand, and things seemed to be running smoothly.

As the morning came around, I arose, still half dozing and reached for my phone. On turning it on, the phone began ringing off the wall, almost burning up with messages from friends needing lifts and directions and, of course, the media from all over Ireland and afar, looking for soundbites and interviews. From very early morning until late that night, I gave live interviews. Early morning started with BBC Good Morning Ulster, then with Frank Mitchell of UTVs u105 top commercial radio show, speaking to every radio station as I attempted to get ready at the same time. With my phone and charger never out of my hand, I continued to speak to anyone who was interested in what was taking place. It was a historic event and one which had not ever happened before in Stormont's Parliament Buildings; hence there was quite a lot of media from home and abroad showing interest in what was about to take place.

On our journey to Stormont and nearing the long driveway to parliament buildings, we noticed that an RTE film crew from Dublin had been waiting on the roadside in a lay-by. On seeing us get out of the car, they proceeded towards us, asking for a live interview and film footage of us walking towards the main building with its long pillars in the rainy background. These large, tall pillars seemed to hold the building up from the outside, though ironically, something miraculously stronger would be needed to hold the politicians within. As in the past and the coming years ahead, it would collapse again and again - this collapse mainly from those in the inside!

RTE Live was broadcast throughout all of Ireland, showing us walking together to Stormont parliament buildings for our apology process to begin, many of us never wanting to see the building ever again. Great feedback was given after that interview, with people getting in contact throughout the whole of Ireland giving their support and their thanks that we had got to this stage and how we had told the world the truth about what had gone on for many years, behind the closed doors in these institutions.

On walking to the front door, where we had entered Stormont for many years, we were stopped and told we were not allowed to enter but instead to access the building through a side door. I did not want to do this, preferring to walk into the building as I usually did through the front door. So, after a little debate around this dispute at the security desk, the manager who had got to know me for many years of travelling up to Stormont, appeared from nowhere, most likely on hearing by phone that there was a bit of a commotion at the side door.

He nodded to me and told the security staff that he personally would walk us up to the front door and into the main hall! He and the other staff members had seen us there so often, and on the news telling our stories of attacks and assaults. They probably guessed and understood our dislike of officialdom.

Many of them, through getting to know our background, respectfully understood our situation and what we had been fighting for. And so it was; we went in through the main front doors, not the small side or back doors. There was a huge significance in doing so. I didn't want to feel like we were being hidden or that our mission was being minimalised in any way. Perhaps that was a trigger on my behalf; most likely it was, as I think back.

On waving our hellos to the police officers and those at the security desk, we entered the large sandstone governmental building this place that I no longer feared. We were given our identity lanyards as usual at the security desk on entry and asked to put them on, as security was still a vital part of this place. It is a government building with high profile politicians walking around at will, hence the need for identity checks, especially here in Belfast.

On leaving the security desk and walking up towards the main hall steps, we immediately found dozens of journalists and news reporters were hanging around with cameras at the ready. They had made sure to be early, so they were prepared and waiting for the day ahead, and from the moment of walking into the building, it was all systems go. Many had already been led upstairs by extra staff put on especially for the day and directed into rooms set aside for us all. I needed and wanted to stay downstairs in the main hall. I was certainly not going to be positioned in an allocated room upstairs out of the main hall, put under observation by our minders.

The longing at this stage was to make sure everything was, at last, finalised, if only to get to the end of the long road of a never-ending campaign of practically harassing and haranguing politicians and authority figures to do their job and to deliver the full findings of the Inquiry. I, for one, had no time to sit down. My mission was to tell the world what had happened to us as children and once again as adults. I wanted to be standing just inside the front doors as I waited on others arriving at the great hall at Parliament buildings, knowing it was necessary to greet people and to reassure them all would be fine. Many had travelled from the UK and various other places to be here on this day. I had seen people gathering who had only wanted an apology, nothing else. They needed to be here for this special healing moment in their lives. I met former ex-residents whom I hadn't seen for many decades. This was also the first time we had met with our social media contacts face to face, victims who had made contact over the years, but we had never met beforehand. That, in itself, was very emotional, especially for others to meet with each other again after such a long time apart.

It was when my brother Kevin arrived that I was then happy and contented. He had been escorted from his nursing home by his kind and caring staff for the occasion. It was more important to me that he would get here in time, as I had been watching out for him in between my conversations. He was upset on seeing this somewhat threatening-looking large government building, thinking it was a courthouse and had to be reassured that it wasn't, again having to tell him that he was going to receive an apology by the highest government authority in the land because of wrongdoing to him and many others. This settled him for a while, though every five minutes, he wanted to get out as quickly as possible for a cigarette. Even as we sat in the chamber, Kevin couldn't cope with sitting still in front of all these people, still believing it was a courthouse.

I realise now that the building triggered him, too, bringing back memories of his last occasion free in the world when a magistrate's courtroom assigned him to Muckamore Abbey Hospital. This day was for him and many others whom I had spoken about previously. This day was for the people who wholeheartedly wanted and needed to see high profile authoritarians, church and religious orders figures put in the dock as it were, standing up in this large arena and apologising to them for the damage and ongoing suffering they had to endure whilst in their care.

What was more meaningful to them was that they *had* to apologise whilst surrounded by so many former abuse victims, politicians, and dignitaries, and all this whilst all from far and away were staring at them either in this main assembly building or from the televisions in the surrounding rooms and from their living rooms across the world, all filmed live on national and international television. It was almost time for all of those who had a specific seat in the main assembly chamber to go take their place in the seats where politicians normally sat when doing parliamentary business, whilst others sat in outer overflow-prepared rooms.

I was still downstairs chatting to university academics and media friends when the former secretary of state for Northern Ireland, Julian Smith, walked through the corridor. On noticing him, I shouted over to the camera crews, telling them that Mr Darcy was on the way and coming towards us. This was the name I had given him from the first day I had met him in Stormont Castle with his officials. He looked and sounded like a distinguished perfect English gentleman, polite and mannerly, akin to those from the film Pride and Prejudice. As we shook hands, the cameras turned towards us, lights flashing all around, my laughter mingling with the giggles of others around me, the media folk, politicians and even the security staff...because of my calling him Mr Darcy.

I had invited the former Secretary of State for Northern Ireland, Julian Smith, to be at the event because I felt he was the only one out of three previous Secretaries of State before him who had wholeheartedly followed through on helping to get the HIA Inquiry findings delivered and legislated on. Others present were MLA Mike Nesbitt, a UUP politician and former UTV news broadcaster, who was always on call and ready to speak out on our behalf in Stormont. Mike was also the chair of the NI Assembly Committee overseeing parliamentary business. He was able to scrutinise and question the roles of the Executive Office along with other civil servants and politicians, asking them for updates in holding them to account.

I was always grateful to Professor Deirdre Heenan, a high-profile academic from Ulster University who took part in the Spotlight programme providing her analysis on why the religious orders in Nazareth House convent were apparently so wicked and uncaring and blatantly dismissive, towards children under their care. Deirdre did this at the request of BBC Producer of Spotlight Darragh McIntyre, with an air of knowledge and knowhow. Deirdre is a professional expert in her field and a learned experienced sought-after contributor to many conferences and to any and all media current affair programmes. We invited these two to be present also.

Unfortunately, the HIA Inquiry Chairman, Sir Anthony Hart, passed away not ever seeing his findings of the Inquiry being delivered, with his passing leaving us shocked and upset. We had respected him in particular for seeing the Inquiry through to the end, delivering for us the findings we had hoped for. He listened to our harrowing records of events which we had endured for many years as children, and came to the right and just decision that what we went through was indeed systemic abuse. He, at last showed us some mercy by staying the course with us, vindicating us and believing our stories, when all before him refused to do so. When no one else believed, he did, in the evidence set before him at the HIA Inquiry.

We wanted to remember him on this day by making sure his dear wife, Lady Mary Hart, would have a seat along with Former Secretary of State Julian Smith in the main assembly chamber. Not ever forgetting former SDLP leader Carmel Hanna and her Special Advisor Anna Mercer/McAllister, who had been the first people to ever listen to me, who, all those years ago, believed me as I let them read my letter that I had written to the sisters of Nazareth asking why they had been so cruel and abusive whilst I was in their care as that very young child. Many others who supported us throughout the campaign were there, gathered in the overspill rooms, which had been fitted with large TV screens just upstairs from the chamber and overlooking the main downstairs hall, which was packed with media correspondents and journalists.

Covid distancing was still in place, so the seating area wasn't available to all who we would have liked to have been present. Those who couldn't attend were able to view the day's events in other stadiums around any of the main cities here in Ireland and the UK and abroad. Claire McKeegan, our solicitor and friend and our campaign court case human rights lawyer, stood close by as always, along with our faithful media reporters and journalists who had become friends over the many years of reporting, Claire Simpson, Allison Morris, Amanda Ferguson, and Chris Page. Chris is the first-ever journalist to report on BBC1 UK on the abuse coming out of the two institutions in which my siblings and I had been placed in Belfast Nazareth House and Rubane House, Co Down.

Whilst all had now made their way to their seats in the chamber, I had waited just outside the entrance with my phone on and tuned into BBC Talkback midday news programme, waiting on the 12.00noon news bulletin to go over, before the lead story on the apology was ready to be aired live. Today's event was to be covered from start to finish throughout the whole delivery of the apology and the speeches from the five Departmental Ministers. I had to keep my promise to a top and well-respected BBC Radio Ulster broadcaster, William Crawley, whom I had got to know so well over the years. He, too, had given me much of his time, allowing me to speak out, calling on the Northern Ireland government to get back up and running and to do their jobs to the very best of their ability. I messaged William and so many others non-stop on TV and radio to ask if they would invite me on to their shows or else to contribute if that day's stories were related to the state of the Northern Ireland Assembly and its collapse. Today, the day of the apology, was no exception. I promised William and his team I would speak to him at noon, and this I did. So, even though all were taking their seats waiting on the ceremony to start, I was talking to William live, his show having a very large reaching audience of all radio programmes in Northern Ireland and beyond.

On finishing talking on the radio, I was motioned by my friendly Northern Ireland Executive Official, Patrick, that I must immediately get into the chamber. It was all about to start with introductions and a run-down of the afternoon's agenda, the speeches and the state of play.

It was the start of a tiring day, a day we had long awaited to arrive and now it was really finally happening. This gave much relief to those who wanted the apology above all else. This was their day to celebrate. For myself, it was to bring an end to the long process and, of course, to see those in authority put through the ropes and to be named and shamed for all to see here in Ireland and throughout the world. On the eleventh of March 2022, the long-awaited day would come when the HIA Apology would take place and be broadcast all around the world.

The apology would be delivered firstly from five departmental Ministers, one from each of the five main lead parties on behalf of the state. It started with them all individually speaking from a heartfelt, sensitively prepared statement apologising on behalf of the state who had let us down all those years ago. Various branches of the Religious Orders would follow by delivering their apology, this coming from the De La Salle Order of the Christian Brothers, the Sisters of Nazareth and the Sisters of Mercy, Good Shepherd Sisters. Those also to apologise were representatives from the Church of Ireland and Barnardos, a children's charity.

When the nuns and the Christian brother read out their statement from an obviously well-prepared and lawyer-protected script, their voices brought back instant memories; whether this was the brogue or dialect, the tone, or the body language, each individual transcribed speech sounded empty and hollow, false, insincere, disingenuous. They lacked genuine warmth. Even though these nuns present were not the nuns of yesteryear, they still belonged to the same establishment and congregation of the Religious Orders in Ireland. The Christian Brother assigned to give the apology on behalf of the De La Salle Order, which ran Rubane House in Kircubbin, Co Down, also stood reading from a prepared legal document, uttering meaningless words with, I felt, not one ounce of authenticity or genuineness.

I believe the majority of the audience had the same feeling in return, all muttering to ourselves, asking just when will this agonising invalid attempt to apologise end. Many had left at this stage because of the harm the lack of healing that the ineffectual apologies had on us. Kevin, my brother, had long removed himself from the chamber, having been escorted by the victims and survivor's services who had been seconded to the arena for the day, thankfully. The sound of insincere voices, the dull, dreary monotone, had taken its toll on him also. He said he was feeling sick, rubbing his tummy as he sat crookedly on the edge of his seat, obviously in anguish. He needed to be freed from this building too. Suddenly, as all had finished reading their apology scripts...it was over. All left the chamber quicker than they entered it. Noticeably, certain people had left swifter than others, using a door entrance at the other side of the chamber. That was it. Now, it was time to go and face the cameras and all the journalists who had been waiting beneath in the long main hall.

After gathering those of our people who had accompanied us this day from the upstairs room where they had coffee, scones, and sandwiches, we headed towards the stairs which led to the main hall below, leading to the front door. This is where we found many more of our team who had congregated outside, many in tears. Kate, my dear friend and comrade, had Kevin by the arm, holding him up to steady his feet.

On noticing this and his tiredness, his nurse, who came along with him, took him out to the car bringing him back to his now more calming setting. He was happy enough in this new place.

We walked towards the cameramen who had been there from early morning. Now that the event had ended, they all waited for us to assemble and to give our thoughts and commentary as to what had just taken place in the chamber. Immediately upon speaking, I had said what took place today was what many wanted. It helped many to be released somewhat from the years of pain, blame and shame they had carried, blaming themselves for what had happened to them as young children and who had lived and carried the stigma throughout their lives of being in an institution that abused them. We agreed the apology from the five departmental leaders of government had been welcome and, we felt, was genuine. But, as for the words of the religious orders, with the greatest respect, we did not believe a word of the apology they had given, telling the media gathered that we would take what they had just uttered with a pinch of salt.

Meanwhile, my dear friend, former City Hall councillor Tim Attwood, had organised a get-together nearby in Horatio Todd's restaurant, supplying food and drinks for all. Tim had supported Kate and me throughout our campaign and was always so generous with his time and kindness. He and MLA Mike Nesbitt, along with Former Secretary of State for Northern Ireland, Julian Smith, were already in the restaurant waiting for me to get there. So, along with Anna Mercer, Claire McKeegan and the gang who had been part of the long fight for justice, we all left Stormont parliament buildings, happy that we had got to the end of the Hart Inquiry findings. With most of my interviews finished, I left Stormont, thankful it would be for the last time in connection, at least, with the HIA Inquiry Campaign. One more live interview, and I was free to celebrate. Channel 4 was waiting to connect to a live broadcast in the outside pub garden of Horatio Todd's Restaurant close by.

I thanked many of the journalists and the cameramen and women who had relentlessly covered our campaign for all those years. In particular, I sincerely wanted to thank Claire Simpson of the Irish News, who was on call

24/7 along with Allison Morris, Irish News, both of whom now are with the Detail and the Belfast Telegraph. Seanin Graham, Irish News was now with The Irish Times. I applauded Chris Page, the BBC UK journalist who broke the story in 2008/2009.

We thanked Darragh McIntyre, Spotlight Investigative Journalist for his Exposé, 'Who is going to say Sorry.' The BBC's Tara Mills, who was always genuinely caring and gave up her time, as we took our campaign to the High Court and won was mentioned. Tara stood outside in the wind and rain with her cameramen and many others, filming the outcomes of every event or protest we held, giving us the headlines, which helped our campaign on every occasion. Mark Davenport, Jayne McCormack, Stephen Walker, Seamus McKee, Claire Savage, Jane Loughery, Tracey McGee, Paul Clark, Mark Mallett, Barbara McCann, Sharon O'Neill, Sarah Jane Clarke, and so many others from UTV. U105s Frank Mitchell, Robert Ainsley and his team, RTE, Cool FM, Q Radio, Radio Ulster, Declan Harvey, William Crawley, Chris Buckler, Joel Taggart and so many other journalists belonging to many media outlets who helped us in getting us to where we are today - photographers included!

Thank you, you all know who you are. Fifteen years, or more, of campaigning for Justice, for Survivors and Victims of Institutional Abuse (SAVIA).

None of you are forgotten. All of you are remembered. I did this for you.